Have you ever felt like leaders you're truly making a lasting impact? In *The Leader's Table*, Gillian Cameron masterfully reminds us that leadership isn't about hierarchy—it's about hospitality, invitation, and transformation. With rich biblical insights and practical wisdom, she challenges us to build spaces where connection and discipleship thrive. This book is a must-read for anyone longing to lead with greater purpose, authenticity, and relational depth.

— **Craig Groeschel**
Senior Pastor, Life.Church and author of *The Benefit of Doubt*

I have known pastor Gillian Cameron, and her husband John for over 25 years. They are two of the most prolific ministers of the gospel and builders of the church of Jesus Christ of our time.

This "must read" book is an essential tool for anyone involved in church leadership, in ministry and in the pastoring and discipling of people of all ethnicities and backgrounds. The principles shared in this great book are universal and proven.

Gillian draws from the deep wells of faith she has dug over the decades, from building ARISE, a mega church that numbered in the tens of thousands from its humble beginnings in a performing arts center with just 35 people. Navigating the highs and lows, the successes and mistakes, the lessons learned and the pains experienced make this book more than just a wonderful read, but a tremendous resource to draw encouragement, strength, faith and courage.

I wholeheartedly endorse this book to anyone aspiring to do something great for the kingdom of God with their lives!

— **Jürgen Matthesius**
Lead Pastor, Awaken Church, San Diego CA

Thousands of books have been written on Christian leadership and just when you think all angles have been exhausted, here comes my friend Gillian Cameron with a totally fresh application of biblical leadership in *The Leader's Table: Unlocking the Power of Relational Discipleship*. You'll read it, teach it, and share it with all your leader friends.

— **Sam Chand**
Leadership Consultant and author of *Leadership Pain*

Gillian Cameron has poured years of wisdom, leadership, and heart into *The Leader's Table,* a book that captures the essence of what true discipleship looks like. With depth, warmth, and practical insight, she reminds us that leadership is not about standing above people but walking alongside them—investing, empowering, and making room for others. This book is an essential read for anyone who desires to build a leadership culture that is both relational and transformational. Gillian's wisdom will challenge and inspire you to lead with authenticity, generosity, and the heart of Jesus.

— **Mark Varughese**
Senior Leader, Kingdomcity and Author of *Ready, Fire! Aim*

A long-time friend of ours, Pastor Gillian has an amazing gift for leading leaders, and a passion to see the next generation of leaders anointed and empowered. Her new book is ripe with nourishment and practical advice on how to draw out the leadership potential in others, create an atmosphere where leaders can flourish, and set the table to put Jesus front and centre. You'll be inspired and encouraged to carry your leadership load with purpose, empathy, integrity, vision, and a servant-heart—guided always by the leading of the Holy Spirit. Be led and fed as you sit around the table with Gillian.

— **Pastors Paul and Maree de Jong**
Founding Pastors, LIFE (New Zealand and Australia)

Gillian Cameron's *The Leader's Table* is a masterclass in relational discipleship, weaving biblical wisdom with real-world leadership insights. With a rich and engaging narrative, she invites readers to embrace leadership that is deeply personal, transformational, and rooted in community. This book is a must-read for anyone seeking to lead with authenticity, wisdom, and the heart of Christ.

— **Samuel Rodriguez**
Lead Pastor, New Season Church and author of *Your Mess, God's Miracle!* President/CEO of National Hispanic Leadership Conference

The Leader's Table is a must-read for church leaders seeking wisdom, strategy, and spiritual depth. Whether you are a seasoned pastor or an emerging leader, this book will empower you to lead effectively and serve with purpose. A transformative guide that will inspire and strengthen leaders at every level.

— **Rich and DawnCheré Wilkerson**
Lead Pastors, Vous Church, Miami, Florida

Leadership isn't just about strategy; it's about connection. In *The Leader's Table,* Gillian Cameron masterfully unpacks the power of relational discipleship, showing that the most transformative leadership moments don't happen in boardrooms but around tables. This book is a must-read for anyone who wants to lead with authenticity, build a culture of discipleship, and create spaces where people grow in faith, purpose, and calling. Gillian doesn't just write about leadership—she lives it. Pull up a seat, dive in, and prepare to be challenged, encouraged, and inspired.

— **Chris Durso**
Author of *The Heist*

As a friend and a co-laborer in the kingdom, I have been blessed to know Gillian for almost thirty years. True leaders lead by example, and Gillian's revelations on leadership and the importance of the table are not just theory but truths and lessons she has learned on the ground and lived out in her own life every day!

Gillian and her husband John are without a doubt two of our generation's most prolific leaders. They are devoted disciples and disciple-makers, and they are culture shifters! The work they accomplished for the kingdom of God across the nation of New Zealand continues to have a profound impact to this day!

Gillian has a unique ability to inspire people of every age and every stage . . . her work with women, men and young people coupled with her strength, wisdom and authenticity, make her a well-rounded and worthy role model for leaders and aspiring leaders to learn from!

Congratulations Gillian on this absolutely magnificent book. It will bring much-needed vision, wisdom and faith to a new generation of kingdom leaders!

— **Leanne Matthesius**
Lead Pastor, Awaken Church, San Diego, CA

THE
LEADER'S TABLE

Empower Leader.

in collaboration with
Torn Curtain Publishing
Auckland, New Zealand
www.torncurtainpublishing.com

© Copyright 2025 Gillian Cameron. All rights reserved.

ISBN Softcover 978-1-991299-48-2
ISBN Hardcover 978-1-991299-51-2
ISBN ePub 978-1-991299-49-9
ISBN Audiobook 978-1-991299-50-5

No portion of this book may be reproduced, stored in a retrieval system or transmitted in any form or by any means—electronic, mechanical, photocopy, recording or otherwise—except for brief quotations in printed reviews or promotion, without prior written permission from the author.

Words or phrases of scripture typeset in bold indicate the author's own emphasis.

Unless otherwise noted, all scripture is taken from the Holy Bible, New Living Translation, copyright © 1996, 2004, 2015 by Tyndale House Foundation. Used by permission of Tyndale House Publishers, Inc., Carol Stream, Illinois 60188. All rights reserved.

Scripture quotations marked NIV are taken from the New International Version®, NIV®. Copyright © 1973, 1978, 1984, 2011 by Biblica, Inc.™ Used by permission of Zondervan. All rights reserved worldwide.

Scripture quotations marked NKJV are taken from the New King James Version. Copyright © 1982 by Thomas Nelson, Inc. Used by permission. All rights reserved.

Scripture quotations marked KJV are taken from The Authorized (King James) Version. Rights in the Authorized Version in the United Kingdom are vested in the Crown. Reproduced by permission of the Crown's patentee, Cambridge University Press.

Scripture quotations marked TPT are from The Passion Translation®. Copyright © 2017, 2018 by Passion & Fire Ministries, Inc. Used by permission. All rights reserved. ThePassionTranslation.com.

Scripture quotations marked MEV are taken from the Modern English Version. Copyright © 2024, 2017, 2014 by United Bible Association. Used by permission. All rights reserved.

Typeset in Minion, Myriad and Agatha Pricilla

Cover photography by Sucin Tan. Used with Permission.
Cover design by Nathan Chambers.

Cataloguing in Publishing Data
  Title: The Leader's Table
  Author: Gillian Cameron
  Subjects: Church leadership, ministry leadership, relational leadership, Christian
    discipleship, hospitality, biblical leadership, team formation, organisational growth.

THE LEADER'S TABLE

Unlocking the power of relational discipleship

GILLIAN CAMERON

To John, one of the greatest leaders in our generation.

I love how much energy and drive you have! It's always exciting to be around you, and a privilege to hear your inner musings. You desire for people to become the absolute best they can be, and you champion others with all your heart. Your belief in me has not only created room for me to flourish but has empowered me to lead from a place of great security and confidence.

You have been consistent in your love for God and in your pursuit of building the Church. Through your relentless determination and unwavering faith, you have impacted the lives of so many people.

I love you, my Scottish red-headed fireball.

THE LEADER'S TABLE

To the Reader		1
APPETIZERS		3
Chapter 1	Dining with Jesus	5
Chapter 2	Reclining at the Table	9
Chapter 3	A Meal with Matthew	15
Chapter 4	A Dinner for Days	19
Chapter 5	Miracles at Mealtime	27
Chapter 6	Inviting Ourselves to Dinner	33
ENTRÉES		39
Chapter 7	A Table of Joy	41
Chapter 8	Secure at the Table	47
Chapter 9	Who's Carrying the Lunchbox	55
Chapter 10	The Centre of the Table	61
MAIN COURSE		69
Chapter 11	Oil on the Table	71
Chapter 12	Anointed at the Table	77
Chapter 13	Freedom is on the Menu	81
Chapter 14	A Leader Worth Their Salt	89
Chapter 15	Waiting on Tables	97

Chapter 16	Serve the Right Food	103
Chapter 17	Try New Recipes. Innovate.	111
Chapter 18	Dine Together, Dream Together	117
Chapter 19	Making Room at the Table	121
Chapter 20	Uncork the Bottle	127

SIDE DISHES 135

Chapter 21	A Table For One, Please.	137
Chapter 22	Complaints About the Menu	143
Chapter 23	Squabbles at Supper	149

SPECIALS 155

Chapter 24	Five Thousand For Dinner? No Problem!	157
Chapter 25	Food in Famine	163
Chapter 26	Dinner With the Devil	169
Chapter 27	Turning Stones into Bread	175

DESSERT 181

Chapter 28	Don't Lose Your Hunger	183
Chapter 29	Expand the Kitchen	189
Chapter 30	Roasting Fish, Restoring Leaders	199
Chapter 31	A Legacy Dinner	203
Chapter 32	It Begins and Ends . . . with Dinner	209

Acknowledgements 211

About the Author 215

To the Reader ♡

I love leadership. I love **to read about it, talk** about it, hear about it, see it in action . . . and to practice it!

My heart's desire in writing this book is to share the things I have observed, learned, and put into practice when leading teams. I pray it enriches your leadership understanding and enables you to grow and become the best leader you can be. If you are already leading a group of people in a church or ministry, you will find in this book a blueprint that will expand your capacity and enable you to become a leader of leaders.

The leadership 'recipes' in this book are based on key spiritual principles that are required of us when leading others with wisdom and love. I pray you are inspired!

THE
LEADER'S TABLE

Appetizers:

CHAPTER ONE

Dining with Jesus

> *Here I am! I stand at the door and knock. If anyone hears my voice and opens the door,* **I will come in and eat with that person, and they with me.**
> Revelation 3:20 NIV

Did somebody say eat?! Back up! *For real? Jesus' first plan for us when we invite Him in is not a list of things we have to do? It's not a task list?* You heard right—it's a meal! It's an invitation to dinner!

I'll never forget the day I opened the door of my heart to Jesus. It was on a sunny winter afternoon at a youth group camp in Auckland. In that moment when I invited Jesus into my life, two things changed. The first was that I was filled with an indescribable joy. The other was that I became hungry! Having been raised in church I knew a lot *about* God, but suddenly I wanted to get to *know* Him. I began to study the Bible and read it deeply, craving to hear what God was saying to me. The Bible was no longer simply words on a page—it was real and alive!

As Jesus began leading me through the scriptures, I started coming alive to my purpose and calling. Day by day, God was shaping and developing a greater understanding of my identity. I was loved! It wasn't about performance—it was about communion with Him. Jesus and I sat together, and as I feasted on His Word and His presence, I began to gain maturity and wisdom. And as a result, my leadership gift began to grow.

As I spent more and more time 'dining with Jesus', I also experienced a dynamic encounter with the Holy Spirit. I had become aware that, although the *fruits* of the Spirit were evident in my life, I was lacking the *gifts* of the Spirit. Deeply desiring to speak in tongues, operate in words of knowledge and the prophetic, and have greater levels of faith, discernment and wisdom, I started by asking for a personal encounter with the Holy Spirit. Right there in my bedroom, in a very special moment, I received the 'baptism of fire' (Luke 3:16). In the days that followed I learned to hear the sound of His voice and treasure His presence, and I began to operate and flow in the gifts of the Spirit. As I leaned into the Holy Spirit's leading, an ease of revelation and understanding came to me. This precious time with the Holy Spirit fundamentally shaped and changed me. It was like I had gained a completely different perspective. I saw life through the lens of eternity, and it heightened my desire to give my all for Him.

Although I was still in school at the time, I began to lead a group of people older and younger than me in studying the Bible. This was a great privilege, and it drove me further into the Bible, fuelling my hunger for more! Continuing to allow Jesus to lead me, I found myself becoming a leader of others.

When Jesus says, "I will come and dine with you," He is expressing something dear to His heart: that feasting together is at the top of his priority list in our relationship with him. Jesus views our relationship with Him as the lynchpin, the way He personally transforms us. I have always been a big fan of food and eating, so if Jesus wants to lead me by eating with me? Hello! Show me to the table!

A meal is the setting Jesus chooses when He enters our lives. Seated with us, He begins His intimate conversations with us. He is not in a rush, He is not ticking us off His 'Lamb's Book of Life list', He's not saying, "Excellent, they have opened the door of their heart, on to the next one." What He wants is to meet with *you*—He desires to come face-to-face with the *real* you! Jesus' goal is for us to become fully mature in our faith, and to change our worldly habits and ways of thinking so we live godly, pure, holy lives. He created us to have a relationship with Him, not a ritual or religion, but the deepest relationship we could ever have. As we come to know Him more, we are transformed into who we were always created to be. We get a deeper understanding of our identity and therefore our purpose.

Eating with us is how Jesus expresses the beginning of His work in our lives. This is very significant. Jesus, the leader of our lives, reveals the central aspect of His leadership—the vital importance to Him of dining and dwelling with us. He loves to sit at a table with us, connecting heart to heart, spirit to spirit. This is significant for every person who wants to make an impact in the lives of others. The way we lead must echo the heart and pattern of Christ.

It is hugely significant that Jesus seeks to sit and dine with us because in His presence we receive revelation. This has an incredible impact on our lives. When Christ reveals something and we respond to it, our faith is increased. As we see things with fresh sight and new understanding, something changes in us. Revelation is not easily lost, because it is hard-won. It always requires an investment of time. It's a commitment.

The intimacy, transparency and revelation that come from 'dining' with Jesus leads to transformation, which in turn empowers our leadership. When we can see more, we can lead with greater authority. Jesus' concern for our growth is the same concern we are to have for those we lead. Likewise, the way He lingers with us and invests in our transformation is the best example of *how* we are to lead.

When we sit at the table with Christ, He develops us and feeds us, sustaining us as we serve Him. When we lead in this way, remaining unhurried and focussed on who we are with, we too can see people flourish and begin to realise their full potential.

During my journey of leadership, I have seen that meaningful connection with others is vital. A true leader desires that each person walks in the fullness of the gifts and calling God has for them. Everyone needs someone who believes in them and takes time with them, encouraging them to be the best they can be. Our investment in people encourages them to do and to *be* more than they ever thought was possible. We must lead in such a way—relationally, from the heart—so that they are empowered, set ablaze and released, and so that in turn they can fulfil their call and purpose for the kingdom.

Developing leadership in others takes an investment of time. Relationships that empower and transform are not microwave meals. How could you linger with those you lead? Are there some key people that you need to spend time with, to go and knock on their door?

CHAPTER TWO

Reclining at the Table

Jesus was incredibly connected to people. In the gospels we find Him connecting with all sorts of people, at unexpected times, and often in situations that felt uncomfortable to His disciples. But the stunning pattern we see throughout His ministry is *where* He connected—how often He was found sitting *at a table*. His entire ministry is intertwined with tables.

Leadership in ministry is intrinsically linked with the act of entering homes and sitting around the table. Jesus did a large amount of His ministry in homes. In fact, one-fifth of Jesus' recorded ministry was carried out in homes. That's massive! Jesus moved around from house to house and village to village—meaning, He sat and reclined at many different tables. He reclined in the house of Mary and Martha, ate lavosh with Lazarus, happily attended dinners with sinners, and hosted a picnic lunch with more than five thousand people! He also arranged an intimate communion supper with His disciples in an upper room, and roasted fish on a simple fire after His resurrection. He even promises us a wedding feast on our arrival to heaven. And this isn't even an exhaustive list. Wherever you find Jesus, you find food! Meals matter to Jesus!

It is amazing to see how many mealtime moments are described in the gospels. For Jesus, meals and ministry went together. Sometimes He did the inviting, and other times He was the guest. Either way, every mealtime with Jesus was significant. At the table with Jesus, people were set free, miracles happened, and perhaps most significantly, Jesus shared what was on His heart. He spoke the most incredible one-liners, and He went intentionally deep. So much of Jesus' teaching was given around meals, along with a lot—I mean, a *lot*—of gritty (or should I say, 'salty') conversations.

Taking time with people around the table was Jesus' pattern for transformational leadership.

He took time to actually *be* with people. People were His purpose. Great leaders are not task-focused, they are people-focused. Leaders carry something that needs to be passed on to others who share their heart. That's why building relationship is so important. When we take our time with people, transformation occurs, truths are revealed, challenges can be given . . . and most importantly, hearts become connected.

Relationships were a core value for John and I as we built the church. We were willing to spend time with people, to share our lives. I truly believe that for John and I, some of our best ministry has taken place around a table.

I see the table as both literal and symbolic. We set a literal, physical table for people to come and sit at. We also create symbolic 'tables' every time we build an environment where people can receive. Throughout His ministry, Jesus tied these together perfectly. In John 21 we see Him lighting a fire on the beach and inviting His disciples to "come and dine." But He was laying a spiritual table as well. When the disciples had all eaten, He offered spiritual growth and maturity to Peter by imparting his life calling—to lead *and feed* others. "Feed my sheep."

Through many years of leadership, one of the most important places where John and I have connected and ministered has been at a literal table, having a meal. The table has been a sacred place for us, a place where heartfelt conversations can take place. Leaders must embrace the importance of creating a table.

From the early days of leading a church, we realised that Jesus didn't just preach to people—He hung out with people. In fact, some of His most powerful preaching flowed out of things He was seeing take place right in front of Him. For this reason, John and I coined the phrase, "We are a hangout church." We wanted church to be more than a meeting or a service. We wanted to truly be a family that could do life together, that could laugh and weep together because we were connected enough to know and share in each other's joy and pain.

Each Sunday during those initial church-planting years we hung out together all day long. I'd have visited the supermarket the day before to buy supplies and then been busy in the kitchen preparing plenty of food for the next day. Those were my 'crockpot glory' days. We only had one morning service, so I would get up early and load the slow cooker so it would be ready when our guests came home for lunch after church. It was wonderful to open the front door and be welcomed by the delicious aroma which was thick in the air by the time we all arrived.

People would come for a bite and stay all day. John would at times sneak off for a quick twenty-minute nap in the afternoon as he was tired from preparing the message and getting up early to lead the setup of the auditorium. (This happened for months, until a friend declared John was not to come so early, that he was willing to shoulder this burden and make sure set-up happened). While John napped during those Sunday afternoons, I would often hold my breath and hope nobody noticed he wasn't there and that they would still enjoy hanging out—but by then, the gatherings had an unstoppable momentum.

As our church grew, we added services, events and meetings, but amidst our growing list of priorities we continued to have people over for meals and to go out for meals. Meals and 'reclining together' were things we consciously strove to keep doing. People who visited our church were often amazed by the friendly and warm culture of our team and congregation, and when they asked how we created this hangout culture, the answer was very simple: we understood the value of spending time with others—and we didn't just ask and expect our leaders to invest in others; John and I also did it ourselves. We modelled the leadership style we wanted to inspire in our team, and the culture caught on. Like Paul, we believed in the power of "you should imitate me, just as I imitate Christ" (1 Corinthians 11:1). We were following Christ's pattern for building leaders and it wasn't a chore, it was a joy. As a result, our team soon became our closest friends. I've often been asked, "Is it a good idea for the people you lead to become your friends?" Our answer is, "Yes, it absolutely is!"

Of course, this comes with its challenges. As our team grew, maintaining our hangout culture wasn't easy and we didn't always get it right. In leadership, there isn't enough energy or time to enjoy the same level of intimacy with everyone. There's only so much of you to go around. What we did was to invest time in key leaders who would go and do the same. We raised up others who had spiritual authority, recognised their ministry giftings, and gave away key ministry duties in public so more people were seen as pastors than just us. We were being stretched thin, and to minister to more people we had to empower and give authority to others who could carry out the duties of the ministry. We did this without second-guessing them.

For John and I, we chose to invest our time with the following people:

- Leaders of other ministries and churches. We always wanted to build up and encourage those who were building the kingdom in different ways than us.
- People who carried large responsibilities within our church. They needed to know our hearts, and we needed to help them with their leadership load.

- People who needed to be called into ministry. We encouraged them in their calling and 'fanned into flame the gift of God', laying hands on them in prayer.
- People who had been with us from the beginning, both peers and friends who we were personally doing life with.
- Church members going through a high-level challenge who needed supernatural breakthrough.

Through reclining and eating with others, we developed camaraderie, communion, connection and lasting friendships. At the table, dreams were breathed into life. But the key for us was to always be ready to dine with someone unexpected, to see the leadership potential in everyone we met. Jesus did exactly that. He reclined and dined with the people that others overlooked.

CHAPTER THREE

A Meal with Matthew

As leaders, we tend to want to work with other leaders and those we see as influential, in order to maximise our time and multiply our fruitfulness. But if we are to recline as Jesus did, this means having way fewer filters around who we hang with than we may think. Jesus clearly spent the majority of His time with His disciples. Most of them came from 'interesting' backgrounds, yet they were transformed as they hung out with Jesus.

We need to be careful to keep our eyes open to who God may want to work through, people we may otherwise disregard. We need to not just choose leaders we think are worthy but allow the Holy Spirit to lead us to those we might ordinarily fail to notice. I wonder if this is why we are told in Hebrews 13:2 that by hosting a stranger we could possibly be entertaining an angel? We never know who we may actually be inviting to dinner!

Pastor Eddie Vargas tells the story of a nine-year-old boy in his youth group named Diga Hernandes who came to him saying that throughout the night he kept feeling the power of God and that the Holy Spirit was giving him visions where he saw himself preaching. In that moment, Pastor Eddie didn't overlook the boy because of his age—he took him seriously and even created an opportunity for this young boy to preach in the youth group. Today, Diga has a huge public ministry. He inspires believers, teaching, preaching and ministering all around the globe in the power of the Holy Spirit. He carries a powerful anointing to see people delivered, healed, set free from addictions, and released to fulfil their kingdom purpose. When we follow the prompting of the Holy Spirit, our leadership impact multiplies.

- It is not always the obvious people Jesus chooses to become leaders.
- He reclined with the unexpected.
- He reclined with the rejected.
- Everyone and anyone could recline with Jesus.

Reclining, lingering, connecting, *where did Jesus find the time?*

The only explanation is that He stayed in step with His Father. He saw people as His Father in heaven saw them. And as a result, He saw people with potential wherever He went. Matthew the tax collector is our Class A exhibit for this. Matthew 9:9-13 says:

> *As Jesus passed on from there, he saw a man called Matthew sitting at the tax booth, and he said to him, "Follow me." And he rose and followed him. And* **as Jesus reclined at table** *in the house, behold, many tax collectors and sinners came* **and were reclining with Jesus and his disciples.** *And when the Pharisees saw this, they said to his disciples, "Why does your teacher eat with tax collectors and sinners?" But when he heard it, he said, "Those who are well have no need of a physician, but those who are sick."*
>
> Matthew 9:9-12 ESV

A MEAL WITH MATTHEW

Matthew, a despised tax collector and sinner, reviled and hated by society, was able to become one of Jesus' closest disciples. Imagine Matthew's huge surprise when Jesus invited him to follow Him. *What, me?! Surely He doesn't mean me?!* But Jesus wasn't looking at the outside of the book—He had opened the cover and read the pages! He knew who Matthew truly was because He had created him! He saw the gold in him, and the very next step of Matthew's discipleship journey, after Jesus called him to follow Him, was to sit down and have a meal with him.

Jesus showed the way to interact with hearts was through intimacy and connection. There were people Jesus sat and shared meals with many times. But often Jesus only ate with people once—only *lingered* with them once—yet there was incredible impact from it because every meeting with Him was a genuine encounter that dramatically changed a life. People were seen. They were understood. They were known and personally ministered to as an individual.

> *Tax collectors and other notorious sinners often came to listen to Jesus teach. This made the Pharisees and teachers of religious law complain that he was associating with such sinful people—**even eating with them!***
> Luke 15:1-2

By eating with tax collectors and sinners, Jesus broke society's rules. A 'good' Jew would never choose to associate with a person like Matthew, even in private, and to make matters worse, at this particular dinner, Matthew invited many other tax collectors to dine with Jesus as well.

Sometimes, our familiarity with the gospels means we don't see just how revolutionary and radical this truly was. What Jesus did here became a topic of discussion; it was a contentious issue. Today we may not be biased by the same issues, but even so, we need to be careful not to let religious prejudices get in the way of seeing the potential leaders among us.

Who we include, we influence. Leadership is about positively influencing as many people as possible. Jesus ate with sinners because He knew that being part of their life and their world could have an impact far beyond who was in the room. Jesus knew that influence and change came from being present with people—even the unexpected ones.

Are we willing to look at those who are not yet mature in their walk with God and invest in them? Jesus ministered to the crowds, but He singled out the ones who were marked for kingdom influence. Let's not just look at people through our natural eyes but with spiritual eyes. Get good at listening to the Holy Spirit when you are around people. Don't miss the prophetic unction. Recognise when someone is carrying leadership in their spirit. They might be right in front of you!

CHAPTER FOUR

A Dinner for Days

What we impart to leaders around our table has the potential to sustain them for many years to come. When Jesus was with those He was developing into leadership, He didn't just give them a fleeting glimpse of His glory—He gave them something lasting and eternal. He gave them a dinner for days. Around the table, Jesus supplied His followers with affirmation, identity, authority and purpose. He gave leaders food for a lifetime.

Just as when we eat, our bones store up and retain deposits of minerals that can later be released when they are needed, those we lead need our wisdom and impartation stored up ready to use in the ministry that lies ahead of them. At the table, we make a rich deposit into their lives, ensuring they have a strong backbone for all God is calling them into. The table is where lasting impartation occurs, where leaders are set up for the future God has for them.

Jesus modelled this beautifully for us when He sat with His disciples at the Last Supper. Far from being a farewell meal, Jesus was imparting everything they would need on the other side of the cross. He knew that what He relayed to them over that meal would be foundational to the establishment of the early church. As He washed their feet, offered them bread, and reclined with His disciples, Jesus was doing more than just preparing them for His departure. He was setting them up for their future ministry.

In appointing the disciples to leadership, He intentionally imparted two things: identity and authority.

An Impartation of Identity

In John 13:14-17 we see that Jesus wanted His disciples to be sure of who they were. He wanted them to know the various facets of their identity: they were to live as sons, they were to be servant-hearted to others, and as a group, they were to be defined by their unity.

Jesus imparted sonship. He wanted the disciples to know first and foremost that they were sons. He told them that they always had a place with Him, that He would not abandon them, that they were loved and valued. They were not going to be 'orphaned' when He left but would be entrusted to do even greater things. He showed them that they belonged to Him and He to them (John 14:21). He centred them in His love. The disciples knew beyond a shadow of a doubt that the love they had for Christ was reciprocated toward them. This love of the Father was to be the foundation in their heart and soul, the source from which their ministry would overflow.

The next important part of their identity Christ imparted to them was servant-hearted leadership. Jesus washed His disciples' feet to show them their identity was found in their humility. They would only be great leaders when they could get to the place of humility, where how others viewed them was insignificant to them. It was to be all about how they saw and valued others, not about how others saw and valued them.

Their identity would never come from the praise of those in the world; quite the opposite. Jesus wanted them to be clear that their worth and value could not be measured rightly by the world: "If the world hated me, it will hate you" (John 15:18). Their identity would not be found in the praises of men;

their success and esteem would not come from the accolades and adoration of people. They had to know that just because the world might hate or demean them, it would never be an accurate gauge of who they truly were.

Around the table, Jesus not only imparted their personal value, He imparted identity to them as a group. The disciples' connectedness, their love and unity with each other, was going to be a key part of their identity. "By this all people will know that you are my disciples, if you have love for one another" (John 13:35). He was showing them that their love for each other would be a defining trait of who they were. If they were going to reflect the nature of Christ, this would be the spirit they would carry. They were to stay united, outworking kingdom purpose with one another. At the core of who they were, they were not independent individuals, they were interdependent kingdom carriers.

An Impartation of Authority

As well as identity, Jesus imparted authority to His disciples. In Luke's gospel, He says:

> *I confer on you a kingdom, just as my*
> *Father conferred one on me.*
> Luke 22:29

Why did the disciples need authority? To fulfil their God-given assignment:

> *I chose you and appointed you that you should go and*
> *bear fruit and that your fruit should abide.*
> John 15:16 ESV

Up until this last dinner with Jesus, the disciples were reliant on following His leadership. They saw themselves as Jesus' helpers, carriers of His ministry. But a distinct transition is taking place during this impartation at the table. Jesus is appointing them to fulfil a role *without Him being physically present*. But they will continue to build God's kingdom—and for that, they need to carry a greater level of authority. Jesus is changing the way they see themselves—and what they believe they are capable of. It's their turn to take the lead. They are the ones who will do greater things in Jesus' name. He tells them they *will* be fruitful, that this work they will do for God will be enduring. Jesus wants them to know with confidence that all their sacrifice and labour will be worthwhile. In putting His endorsement on them, Jesus is giving His disciples certainty about their calling and is letting them know that He has personally chosen them.

As leaders, knowing that God has given us an assignment is a powerful way to live. So often we can think, "Who am I to be doing this?" Or "Who do I think I am?" These are self-doubts that leaders often hold. But Jesus imparted His faith and belief in His disciples because He didn't want them to question themselves or their 'rightness' for the role. He wanted them to *know* that He had given them the authority. It could not be questioned.

This was especially important because, before this dinner, the disciples had misguided questions about who was the greatest. They were vying for position and influence, but Christ conveyed to them a revelation of leadership—that it is never about position; it is always about authority. What Christ gave them at this supper was authority. Authority cannot be taken; it can only be given and received. He knew that His disciples needed that strength of conviction. They needed to hold unwaveringly to the knowledge that they were *appointed!*

This impartation would empower the disciples to carry out their assignment. What was being imparted? Strength—the disciples didn't need to second-guess themselves on the day of Pentecost because kingdom authority had already been conferred on them around the table. They had not received a mere moment of comfort at the Last Supper but an impartation that would shore up their position and call for many years to come.

This raising up of leaders who have spiritual authority is vital in the church. But it's important to differentiate between the role of a leader and the role of a manager. Managers tend to put things in order and ensure people are serving in the right places, whereas leaders look for ways to elevate people to new levels. Managers work with what they have right in front of them in the moment, while leaders work with the potential they see in people. Managers lean more on analytical observations, whereas leaders tend to lean on intuition. Managers fulfil an amazing function in seeing plans and processes outworked, but it is the job of a leader to spot a leadership gifting in others. Whenever we get frustrated at a lack of leadership multiplication, we need to remember: it takes a *leader* to raise a leader.

When leaders sit with future leaders, a beautiful transaction of strength and equipping can take place. Like Jesus, they call others to lead by 'sending them' and by appointing them to the work of the ministry. "As you sent me into the world, so I have sent them into the world" (John 17:18 ESV).

An Impartation of Confidence

When we are imparting authority, we need to tell the leaders at our table, "Hold tight to the knowledge that your calling is sure. He has placed His gifts in you and positioned you. If opportunities open up, see that it is God who has opened an effective door of ministry. If you preach, don't question yourself and think you can't share anything great. Remind yourself: *this wouldn't have happened if God hadn't opened the door! God wants me here, so I need to do it in the authority He gives.* The one who prophesies should prophesy as if speaking the very words of God. God wants you to do it. You are a man of God; you are a woman of God; you are anointed and appointed, and your time is now!"

With an impartation of identity and authority, we cement in leaders the confidence to embrace their assignment. This assignment may come with challenges on a physical and spiritual level. As leaders, we can fortify and prepare them for what lies ahead.

At the table during the Last Supper, Jesus turned to Simon Peter and said:

> *Simon, behold, Satan demanded to have you,*
> *that he might sift you like wheat.*
> Luke 22:31 ESV

It's a comfort that Jesus knows ahead of time what we are going to do and what we will go through. Leaders will face fights. Simon Peter needed to know that the attack he would experience was because Satan did not want his potential to be unleashed!

Satan would try to undermine Peter's identity as a rock. But Jesus wants Peter to know that he is going to be one of the future leaders of the church. There's a war over his identity. A reed gets blown over in adversity. Peter so easily sees himself as a reed, not as a rock. Jesus is saying, "Satan will try to treat you like a reed, but I call you a rock. Ultimately you will stand strong." He's imparting the truth of Peter's kingdom assignment. Nothing can thwart the purpose of God—not Peter's own weakness, nor the devil's attack.

Jesus can see our humanity, yet He also sees the spiritual realities, the warfare, and the future challenges we will walk in. And He adds this to His prophetic warning:

> *When you have turned again, strengthen your brothers.*
> Luke 22:32 ESV

Around the table, prophetic warnings do not come without encouragement—they come with a prophetic promise: "You're not just going to survive; you're going to lead others to a place of strength!" Jesus is reassuring Peter that though he is going to fail, that failure is not going to limit his leadership.

This is what emerging leaders need to hear! They may experience momentary weakness, but it is not going to ultimately hinder their effectiveness.

There is something more that Jesus adds, and those of us who raise up leaders need to give them this as well. They need to know that they are not alone. We need to assure them, "The call that's ahead of you—you're going to have to fight to fulfil the purpose of God, but we're going to support you all the way."

When Jesus added, "But I have prayed for you," He wanted Simon to know, "Not only do you have what it takes; I've got your back." Jesus is putting courage into Simon. "You're not going to be alone. I've already prayed for you. This has already been covered in prayer. I'm your shield and rear guard."

> Nothing establishes friendship so forcefully as eating together.
> – Jonathan Safran

As leaders, when we are at the table confirming the assignments of others, we can expect there will be warfare attached. "You have an assignment on your life, but Satan has an assignment against you, too. The warning isn't to cause you to turn aside or head in the other direction." Around the table, we encourage leaders to press forward anyway. "Take a risk. Go ahead, do what is in your heart to do. And—I've got your back. I'm going to pray for you, I'm going to check up on you." The people we lead and love will fulfil their purpose, but it's on us to keep covering them.

After Jesus was gone, a group of people carried the same spirit because it had been imparted to them around the table. The early church followed this pattern of discipling leaders, breaking bread together in homes, appointing deacons, and imparting the heart of God. Believers were given authority and called into ministry.

Jesus understood the power of a dinner to live beyond the moment. Great leaders leave people in surplus. They leave people feeling built up, enlarged, equipped and empowered to take their next step. Great leaders prophesy and prepare people to step into their future with confidence.

If we want to see leaders released, we need to set a table. When I identify an up-and-coming leader who needs a fresh impartation for a new day, I plan a dinner, pray into the situation, prepare an atmosphere, think through what God needs to do in their life, and then look for openings during the meal to raise what God has placed on my heart. Leaders who do this understand that this is the right expenditure of energy—serving others so that they might grow and be enlarged in their spirit.

For a season, one gifted woman visited and was part of our family regularly. She had a mighty talent that we were encouraging her in, but her family life was incredibly difficult. Her father was neglecting and abandoning her, so we brought her into our world to surround her with love and security. We prayed through the hurt and rejection, counselled her, and embraced her with love. Over the course of that investment, it was beautiful to see her ministry gain strength as she became even more sure and confident in herself. As we imparted identity, we were also able to release her into a greater level of authority in her leadership of others.

Great leaders know the value of lasting impartation. We may not be at the same table again, so we make the occasion count. We impart something that is not just momentary. We are creating self-sustaining ministers and ministries. We don't just feed people; we show them how to feed others. The impartation that happens over one meal can flow to people you will never even meet.

Jesus knew that His time was coming to an end, and He chose to dine before His death. What a significant revelation that Jesus' last moments were spent in an intimate meal, conversation, and prayer. His last moments weren't spent preaching to the crowd. Instead, He imparted something lasting to those who would become core leaders of the church.

CHAPTER FIVE

Miracles at Mealtime

Lingering at the table goes far beyond meeting people's relational needs. Lingering together unlocks supernatural moments as well!

We see this in the life of Jesus. Meals and miracles... when Jesus was at the table, they went together. It is no coincidence that it was during a meal that Jesus performed His first miracle.

Notice the setting: Jesus and His disciples had been invited to a wedding at Cana in Galilee. The young couple were about to embark on married life, but already they faced a setback. It was Mary, Jesus' mother, who brought the problem to Jesus:

> *When the wine ran out, the mother of Jesus told him, "They have no more wine."*
> John 2:3

Imagine the embarrassment for this young couple. The wine had been flowing all night long so thankfully, the guests were blissfully unaware of the dilemma. But the bride and groom were panicking. This was a shameful moment for them. The celebration was about to come to an abrupt end. What a failure of hospitality on their part! Suddenly, their reputation hung in the balance. In that moment, they needed more than platitudes—they needed a solution. There was no more money for wine. There was no stash out the back. There was no physical solution. *But Jesus was at their table!*

It was no coincidence that Jesus was a guest at their wedding feast that day. Hearing of their dilemma, Jesus turned to the servants. "Fill the jars with water," He said to them. "... now draw some out and take it to the master of the feast" (John 2:7-8, ESV). The servants obeyed, not in half measure, but after filling the jars to the brim, they went to the master of the feast.

Imagine their relief and joy when they discovered that the water had turned to wine! It was a miracle! Living under Roman oppression meant high taxes and ever-present scarcity. Yet into that scene, Jesus brought abundance. Amongst poor substitutes and desperation, He brought first-class quality, the real thing. He made it look like the couple had intentionally saved the best until last! This wine was, of course, the greatest wine anyone had ever tasted. Their sommelier was astounded. It was so fantastic! And, it was plentiful! Jesus had performed a miracle at their table.

When the miraculous breaks out in a person's life, the result is lasting and has eternal impact. Miracles overflow generationally! The newlyweds received more than a momentary fix, they received a multiplication miracle that would have set them up for their life ahead. Can you imagine what it would be like to have some of that wine passed down through the family? On each special and revered occasion, a bottle would have been opened, and in that moment, the rich aroma of the wine continued to testify to the rich love of Christ for them.

With one miracle, a whole family's future was redefined. They no longer thought of themselves as poor. Christ had touched their life, making everything possible. Their future was filled with hope. Their insecurity had been replaced with confidence and certainty.

Miracles take people out of the uncertainty into the certain.

Keys to Unlocking Miracles

I believe there can be a miracle at every leader's table. When Jesus turned water into wine, lives were transformed through His presence, His compassion, and His readiness to minister in miracles.

1. Be present

I've seen many miracles take place because John and I were present at tables. I've seen broken hearts mended, bodies physically healed, people delivered from demonic bondage, marriages redeemed and rebuilt, spiritual giftings unlocked, prophecies given, and prayers prayed that were "no sooner prayed than answered".

At the wedding feast, Jesus was present—He was there—He was in a place and space where He could do a miracle. He wasn't isolated, He was connected. He was willing to be there in the moment with ordinary, everyday people.

Because Jesus was present, He could connect with the newlywed's problem and minister to the need, transforming their present and their future. Leaders with lives connected to others can be used by God to minister supernaturally. But the supernatural often happens in very natural moments—like around a table. I truly believe there are miracles to be found at tables.

As leaders, when we connect with people in their everyday lives, we get to see where they are really at, and from there, ministry flows—both pastorally and supernaturally. Our 'being present' has the potential to change lives!

2. Be compassionate

At the wedding in Cana, it was the compassion of Christ and His awareness of their deep need for breakthrough that caused Jesus to respond. It is our compassion that connects us with those we lead. When we see the needs of the people around us and feel the pain of those we serve, we are moved to press through on their behalf. We are stirred to rise up in intercession, break through the spiritual ceiling they face, and by faith, pull down heaven's answer for them. Our hearts are moved, and we feel for them—to the point where we are passionate for them to see their miracle.

It is essential as leaders that we recognise moments of compassion as a prompt to lean into what God might want to do in that moment. *Has He got a miracle waiting to be released? Could it be that our faith is meant to unlock that miracle?* We need to recognise the Holy Spirit's unction and leading. There is an anointing in that moment to reach for a miracle.

3. Be ready

As a guest at the wedding in Cana, Jesus was somewhat reluctantly thrust into the public eye. How many of us can relate to this?! In leadership, moments like this often come unexpectedly. All eyes are on you, and you'd better have something of value to say or give!

This is why it is so important for us to stay in tune with the heart of the Father. Like Jesus, we need to keep in step with the Holy Spirit. Before Jesus ever went to the wedding, He was carrying an anointing for miracles. He could do what was needed when it was needed because He was already ready! When the moment for a miracle presented itself, Jesus could supply what was lacking.

This is how leaders need to live! We must always have something from the Holy Spirit ready to give away before it is required. When we connect with people around the table, let's expect miracles to break forth! There are people in our lives who are in great need. But there are also people waiting in the wings, watching to see how we will respond. At the wedding in Cana, Jesus' disciples caught their first glimpse of who Jesus really was and the greatness of the ministry they would be part of. It was not just the couple, but Jesus' disciples, who were forever changed because of this one meal. In John 2:11 (ESV) we read:

> *This, the first of his signs, Jesus did at Cana in Galilee, and manifested his glory. And his disciples believed in him.*

This feast grew the faith of everyone who tasted it. With one miracle, Jesus' leadership influence was established and the disciples' faith was galvanised. As leaders, let's welcome the miraculous, ushering heaven into our moments around the table.

CHAPTER SIX

Inviting Ourselves to Dinner

> *"If you really want to make a friend, go to someone's house and eat... the people who give you their food give you their heart."*
> — Cesar Chavez

The more Jesus connected with people, the more His leadership influence grew. Most times, Jesus was invited to be a guest at someone else's table—whether at the wedding in Cana, the home of Simon, or Lazarus. But when Jesus identified someone who should be part of His kingdom plan, He didn't wait for them to give Him an invitation—He invited Himself! In Luke 19:1-5 we read:

> *Jesus entered Jericho and made his way through the town. There was a man there named Zacchaeus. He was the chief tax collector in the region, and he had become very rich. He tried to get a look at Jesus, but he was too short to see over the crowd. So he ran ahead and climbed a sycamore-fig tree beside the road, for Jesus was going to pass that way. When Jesus came by, he looked up at Zacchaeus*

and called him by name. "Zacchaeus!" he said. "Quick, come down! **I must be a guest in your home today."**

When Jesus saw Zacchaeus looking down at him from the tree, He immediately invited Himself to dinner. Imagine the shock and surprise Zacchaeus must have felt. Zacchaeus was an outcast in that society. He wasn't invited to parties, he wasn't socialising with others, he never realised the leadership potential he carried. He had only heard 'the talk of the town' about this person Jesus, and he wanted to see this man for himself.

Jesus hadn't planned to stop in Jericho. At this moment in His ministry, He is on the clock. He has already set His face to go to Jerusalem (Luke 18v31-33). The countdown to His death is getting closer every hour. But He again shows what He prioritises. In Zacchaeus, Jesus sees something others do not see. He sees something that Zacchaeus himself is not even aware of. Jesus sees a man who is ready to be activated into kingdom ministry.

Leaders step into other people's worlds before they are invited. They involve *themselves*. Jesus says, "Hey! I'm going to come and eat with you, Zac!" Jesus could have called out the potential in Zacchaeus right there on the road, but instead, He invites Himself to dinner. He wants to spend time with Zacchaeus.

Why would Jesus take the time to invest in one individual when He was on His way to give His life for the whole world? *Why not preach some more? Why not pray for more people?* Because Jesus understands that activating a leader is going to achieve more for the kingdom than fulfilling the work of the ministry Himself. He's coming to the end of his ministry yet He's still looking for those to whom He can impart leadership.

What characteristics of a leader did Jesus see in Zacchaeus?

1. He was hungry for more of Jesus

When Zacchaeus heard Jesus was passing by, he didn't stroll, he wasn't being casual—he ran to get a good view! Zacchaeus was *desperate* to see Jesus, and he put in a big effort to do so.

Intentional leadership is about looking for those who have a visible hunger for Christ. This hunger is not something we can give people—it's something the Holy Spirit places within a person. Zacchaeus was a self-made man, but he was no longer satisfied. He was searching for meaning, looking for something more in his life. He was seeking for the presence of God, a move of God, and the power of God. He wasn't happy with more of the ordinary—he wanted the things of heaven in his life.

2. He was innovative

Leaders don't just invite themselves to anyone and everyone's house. They look for people who are not just doing what the crowd is doing, people who stand out from the crowd, people who do things in fresh ways.

Zacchaeus was innovative. He had climbed a tree to see Jesus. Admittedly, he was short, but he found a way to compensate for his disadvantage. This is a characteristic of amazing leaders—they find a way to make things happen. They are 'box-breakers'—they can achieve things by thinking differently. They need us to affirm the leadership gift in them—but we also need their fresh perspectives in our own leadership!

When we discover people who see the world differently or bring a new perspective, it's worth getting around a table together. Maybe that's why the 'roundtable' has always played a pivotal role in history. Something fresh is ignited when leaders sit together.

3. He responded to Jesus' invitation with joy

When Jesus surprised Zacchaeus by inviting Himself to dinner, Zacchaeus was overjoyed. He was excited to be with Jesus! This enthusiasm is what we are looking for in those we are calling out for leadership. We are looking for those who lean in and respond eagerly when we offer our investment in them. There isn't much point investing in people who don't care for what we have to bring.

Look at the people around you. *Is there a sense that they care about and are interested in what you have to say? Do they want to get on the same page as you? Do they like you and what you stand for?* Look for those who express an eager desire to receive discipleship or input from you.

4. He was willing to change

Zacchaeus wasn't reluctant to change—he just needed someone to create the right environment. He needed someone to believe in him, to be recognised and seen. In that atmosphere of acknowledgement, Zacchaeus was quick to embrace change. He was willing to hear and respond to Christ, and as a result, he experienced a total change of priorities.

In kingdom culture, there is a willingness to change. Those we identify as leaders understand they are on a journey. They are willing to be shaped and to grow. They are not clinging to what they have already achieved or accumulated as a person. People may be talented, but if they are proud, relying on and trusting in their personal talents, they may not be the ones God is calling to leadership.

5. He had personal drive

Before he met Jesus, Zacchaeus was motivated to make money. This led to him manipulating and cheating people out of their money. But despite this being terrible behaviour, it revealed something important about Zacchaeus—he had personal drive. He just needed that drive to be redeemed.

When our lives are turned around by Jesus, we don't get a totally different personality or a totally different skill set. Zacchaeus still had the same drive and the same level of motivation, but after being with Jesus, this drive and motivation were directed the right way. He no longer desired wealth for his personal gain; he wanted to use it to put things right. He still saw opportunities, but he saw opportunities for generosity, not for greed. I wonder what the people who had their money returned thought of this? Many lives were impacted by Zacchaeus' newly ignited heart. I wonder if they connected the dots? Did they realise that just one dinner had made the difference?

I believe that along our leadership journey, there will be Zacchaeus's ready to welcome us into their lives if we will take the initiative. Being a leader means that we need to intentionally step into people's worlds. People who are driven and purposeful don't always stop and ask God what their purpose is. But this doesn't mean they are not ready to embrace the leadership He has placed on their lives. They may just need someone to challenge them with the question, "Is this what the Lord has for your life?"

In our church leadership, John and I were attentive to those who displayed an unusual level of spiritual hunger. Perhaps it was the abandon with which they worshipped God, the kindness they displayed towards other people, or the desire they seemed to have to learn about God. These people had great ministry potential. But we noticed in New Zealand that ministry was seldom in people's minds. Even highly anointed people didn't see pastoring or being a missionary as something they could do. There was no obvious pathway for them other than a secular career. A lifetime of ministry wasn't even on the table. And yet we could see the hand of God on their lives, a special anointing, the possibility that if their heart was for ministry we could help them journey towards that.

Like Zacchaeus, some of those we reached out to were quite surprised. Sometimes they were nervous. But as we sat around the table, we watched their excitement begin to grow. They began to see that they could use their God-given gifts and that ministry leadership might be for them! More importantly, they realised that they didn't have to figure it out by themselves because somebody else was invested in their leadership journey.

Many of those we met with went on to become paid pastors in the church and to this day are vibrant and integrous ministers and preachers of the Gospel. We simply needed to see the gift of God in them and create a pathway for them to become ministers.

I'm sure many people looked at Jesus' dinner with Zacchaeus critically. "Of all the people to have dinner with, he's going to eat in the house of a crook," they said (Luke 19:7 TPT). This is understandable. Zacchaeus was not obvious leadership material, not typical company for the Son of God. And yet he was the vessel God wanted to move through.

Let's be ready to look beyond those who invite us in. Let's invite *ourselves* to dinner.

> *Lord, I pray that you would give me the gift of discernment to see the people I need to spend time with. Help me not see them with natural eyes but with your eyes. Jesus, I believe you are going to enable me to lead leaders. Give me the unction to stop and dine where I should. Lead me as I serve in building your Church. Amen.*

THE LEADER'S TABLE

Entrées:

CHAPTER SEVEN

A Table of Joy

Did you know there is a 'proper way' to set a table? Maybe you've seen behind-the-scenes images from the White House or Buckingham Palace. As the staff prepare for a state banquet or grand occasion, they pull out all the stops! The silverware, the porcelain, the crystal glasses are all specially chosen for the occasion. To those of us with regular lives, it can seem a bit 'extra'—but, true confession, I've practised setting the table 'just right'. I've laid out the three different forks, the fancy napkins, the serving platters, the centrepiece. For three years, my mum sourced pieces of a French *'Laguiole'* cutlery set I was collecting to give me as a Christmas present—which is fitting since Christmas is the only time it ever gets used! (Correctly setting the table was nearly as short-lived as my Marie Kondo clothes-folding phase).

Why would we go to the bother of setting the table? It's because we want to provide guests with an amazing experience as they eat. A beautifully laid table is a statement: "I'm expectant about your presence here. This is a table of joy and I've made a space for us to connect."

It is important to set a table for our leaders where they feel special and valued, to create an atmosphere where they can be freshly inspired. So many of our table environments as leaders are strategic. We sit at roundtables, we bring our agendas, we hold planning meetings, we discuss budget and staffing requirements, we meet for organisational reviews... yet leaders are craving a table that offers more than that. A place that feels festive. Special. Fun!

Who can watch the opening scene of *The Hobbit* without wanting to be part of that picture?! It's the epitome of fellowship. As the little company gather before they head out on their grand and risky endeavour, we find them sitting around a table. It's jovial and light-hearted. They're teasing each other, they're relaxing and reminiscing, they're feasting. Their shared purpose has brought them together, and by the end of the night, their spirits are high, their camaraderie is established, and they're ready to take on whatever comes their way.

People need to be invited to tables that are not just dedicated to work. As leaders, we have the privilege of setting tables where people can come together purely for friendship, fun and refreshment. Leaders need the fellowship and joy that can be found at your table because leadership can be hard! There are tough moments in leadership, moments when the reality doesn't match up to the expectations, moments of disappointment, moments when we can't see beyond the current challenges we face. As leaders, it's easy at times like this to end up in a downward spiral. But one meal, one festive, joyful gathering with friends can shift everything. As leaders, we can provide the perfect setting to lift others to a place of renewed positivity. One banquet can restore the wonder of life!

John and I don't always go overboard when we host friends and leaders, but sometimes going a little bit 'wow' in our planning and hospitality has been exactly what was needed. Sometimes it's worth designing a special meal—lighting the candles, arranging flowers, laying the fire... even pulling out the *Laguiole* cutlery!

Maybe it's a family who has been going through a tough time, maybe it's pastors who usually do all the hosting, maybe it's that person who's mostly on their own and doesn't have family nearby. Or maybe it's the people we work

A TABLE OF JOY

alongside who simply need to know, "We enjoy you, we love you, we want to linger with you, not as a colleague, but as a person."

This isn't always about setting a literal table. It's about creating a place and space for people to be ministered to. It's about setting an environment that puts things in perspective and lets people find their joy once more. I remember a time when a leader did this for me. In that particular season, John and I felt like we were going through hell. We were spiritually, mentally, emotionally and physically exhausted. There was nothing left in the tank. And then a leader reached out to us. Over FaceTime we began sharing how we were doing, what we were going through, the fact that it was all very heavy-going. This leader didn't dismiss what we were sharing or play it down. Instead, they did something that completely shifted the atmosphere for us. They began cracking jokes and laughing at how crazy it all was. By the end of the call, we were all laughing together. By the time John and I finished that call, our spirits were lifted. This leader had helped us see that life was not ending, that there is always a future. Their lightheartedness helped us put it all in context. We went away from that call energised because someone had intentionally strengthened us at a table of joy.

This is a spiritual dynamic: "The joy of the Lord is our strength" (Nehemiah 8:10). An atmosphere of joy can produce spectacular growth and impetus in the lives of others. When we create an atmosphere that is life-giving and upbeat, people are revived. This is what being a minister and a leader is all about. It's about raising up and reviving the people we lead. We are to focus on how we can encourage them, help them, and build them up in the Lord and in their faith. We need to 'turn up' for people in a way that lifts them and helps them find renewed joy and enthusiasm. We want our leaders to remember that, despite the challenges, life is good and ministry can be fun!

Jude 1:20 says, "You, dear friends, must build one another up in your most holy faith." People who build others up are those who make the effort to pick up the burdens people throw out there and respond with faith, with a readiness to pray, with an expression of worship ... and sometimes, even with laughter! It doesn't take much to lift people from the valley to the mountain-top. Changing the altitude or atmosphere can change a person's entire outlook. People are drawn to us when we make them feel good, when we remind them of the truth that God works all things together for good, and when we strengthen them with our joy.

> *A merry heart does good, like medicine.*
> *Proverbs 17:22 NKJV*

The truth is, joy is more than a concept—it is something that overflows in merriment and laughter! Laughter has extraordinary benefits. It's good for the immune system, it relieves pain, it improves our mood, it provides connection with others—it can even help us live longer! Good leaders see the whole person and deliberately create environments of laughter and joy.

One of our key church leaders in New Zealand was hosting a group of leaders at her home one night when she noticed that the atmosphere was a little tense. For some reason, everyone seemed a bit cranky. Deciding the mood needed to be lightened, this woman put on an Italian accent, had everybody hold up their plates, and rather than nicely serving up the pasta, she began tossing spaghetti across the room onto their plates. As strands of spaghetti flew through the air like streamers, the room went crazy—soon people were shrieking with laughter and the gloom was gone. Although the clean-up afterwards might not have been pretty, the atmosphere of that crazy, chaotic moment, that moment of surprise, was jaw-dropping. That's the kind of atmosphere that causes people to see the bright side of life!

In all the seriousness of life and ministry, let's not lose our ability to laugh. As a leader, be the one who lightens the mood, who shifts the atmosphere for others. Be ready to tell a funny story. Save silly anecdotes to share.

Most people will enjoy laughing at your expense. Trust me—I have an endless supply of those kinds of stories!

Let's be intentional about creating light-hearted, happy environments for those we lead. When people are at a restaurant and are having a really good time, they tend to stay for dessert. They want to order more! Living in the full measure of joy makes others want more of what we've got. It's contagious. Let's be leaders who cause others to say, "I want to be at that table. It looks like a party!"

CHAPTER EIGHT

Secure at the Table

I'll never regret a decision I made when I was pregnant with our son, Will. I had been invited to preach at a very large youth conference with thousands of attendees. This conference was being held in three different cities and I had been invited to travel to every city it was running in. It was an exciting opportunity, and a dream come true to minister to teenagers on that scale. When I first saw and thought about the invitation, I *really* wanted to say yes. But as I prayed, I got a strong impression that I wasn't meant to do it. I still believed that I was called to preach in that environment, but in prayer, I got the sense that I wasn't ready. It was the right opportunity, but it wasn't the right time. And so I did what seemed crazy—I turned down the invitation to travel and elected to only speak in my home city.

To some, it probably didn't seem like a smart choice, but because I had sat at the table with God, I was secure in His plan for me. I realised that it is possible to birth something in a rush and that moving ahead of God's timing can mean we give birth to an Ishmael, not an Isaac. Abraham tried to make things happen in his timing, not trusting the Lord to produce an heir, and it badly affected the future. For me, speaking on that scale at that point in time would not have been a representation of God's best work in my life. It could also have impacted people's perception of me as a minister. By putting myself out there before I was ready, people would have seen something unformed rather than honed, and I could easily have been written off.

Many years later, I was again asked to speak at that conference, and this time I was ready. A large number of teenagers were saved as I spoke and ministered, and I know that the impact was more significant as a result of waiting. And that wasn't the end of the story—later, the running of the conference was given to myself and John. We became the overseers of it!

God has a funny way of working. When we rest, and don't force or push, God has a way of opening doors for us—often wider than we thought possible! We need to get to the point as leaders where we are no longer trying to carve out room for ourselves at the table because we know there is a place already set for us.

Secure in our Relationships

I love reading about the friendship of Mary and Elizabeth in Luke 1:39-45. These two women exemplified a great sense of their own personal security, loving and supporting each other during a time when they were both experiencing an extraordinary level of God's favour on their lives.

Elizabeth was the older, more mature of the two women. She brilliantly embodies the characteristics of a person who is secure enough in themselves to celebrate and champion another highly-favoured person. Among the twenty thousand priests serving that year, her husband Zechariah's name was drawn by lot to enter the holy of holies to offer incense to the Lord. How amazing! Zechariah is being chosen to do the very thing he had trained his whole life for—and on top of that, he gets an angelic visitation!

This is a miracle on top of a miracle. For the first time in four hundred years, God has spoken, and Zechariah's wife, who has previously been unable to conceive, becomes miraculously pregnant. The surrounding towns must have been abuzz with talk of how exceptional this child must be and what God will surely do through him.

Elizabeth has stepped into a season of very public favour. If ever she has had cause to feel important and special, it is now. Yet she does not feel any need to broadcast what God is doing in her life. Even in the midst of the incredible favour she is experiencing, Elizabeth does not assert superiority. She does not become the centre.

Mary is led by God to stay with her relative, Elizabeth. When Mary walks in, Elizabeth immediately focuses on her. Full of faith, the Holy Spirit, love and prophetic unction, she declares how incredible it is that the 'mother of her Lord' has come to visit her. She even goes so far as to say that she is not worthy of this honour.

Elizabeth is the personification of a secure, Spirit-filled person who God can trust. Mary was in the early stages of her pregnancy, and both she and the pregnancy needed to be nurtured and protected. God entrusted Mary to Elizabeth.

Secure in God's Purposes

Elizabeth understood that she already had a seat at the table in God's purposes and plans and that welcoming another person to take her place at that table was no threat to her. Elizabeth displayed what someone who is seated securely at the table looks like. Let's look at seven characteristics of secure people:

1. Secure people get excited about other people's blessing, promotion, and potential

Elizabeth is secure enough to be excited about what God has done for Mary. She prophesies over Mary. If we want to put it bluntly, what she is essentially saying is, "Your baby is more important than my baby!" This is not the language of an insecure person! An insecure person makes comparisons and talks about their own importance, while a secure person can rejoice in the importance of others. Elizabeth shows that she loves to give praise and honour. She is not seeking praise for herself.

Because she is so secure, she reproduces security. Her ability to honour others, to allow others to be considered greater than her, is echoed in the life of her son, John the Baptist. He understood that Jesus must become greater and that he must become less. He was willing to acknowledge the supremacy of Jesus. John knew his place. He says of Jesus, "He is the one who comes after me, the straps of whose sandals I am not worthy to untie" (John 1:27). Elizabeth modelled security to her son, and we see right from the start of his ministry that John is also secure.

Our security will reproduce the same in others. How beautiful it is that Elizabeth prophesies over Mary, and in turn, Elizabeth's son prophesies over Mary's son!

This is what secure leadership looks like—secure leaders tend and nurture others' callings and speak to them with excitement and selflessness. They love to give praise and encouragement. They are not threatened by the giftedness in others but love to see it and call it out. If we can be this kind of person, God will send leaders to us as their God-given call and destiny are beginning to be formed. A secure leader gets the privilege of releasing that calling in others.

When someone close to us gets a new opportunity, experiences a miracle, or does really well, are we happy for them? Can we say "Well done!" and mean it? Can we rejoice at others' successes? Secure people can!

2. Secure people are happy for others to learn what they know

Have you ever eaten something delicious and thought, *Wow! I really need that recipe!* So you find the person who made it and say to them, "Can I get that recipe?" Perhaps they reply, "Sure, of course you can" ... but then they never send it to you. I don't think that's always because they forgot. I think sometimes people don't want to give away the very thing that they get complimented for. This is exactly why most companies don't share their 'secret sauce' recipe—they want to keep the market share.

Insecure people don't want to feel replaceable or be replaced by others doing what they do. Training others to do what we do is scary, but releasing others is part of our calling. When Mary stayed with Elizabeth for three months, this was a foundational time for her. She saw how to be a godly wife, how to serve others, how to flow in prophetic anointing, how to run a household, how to be a woman of standing, how to endure gossip and speculation, how to hold God's promise in her heart. Elizabeth taught Mary everything she knew.

As leaders, our goal has to be to release others, and part of that involves replacing ourselves by letting others learn what we know.

3. Secure people give away the credit

Insecure people need the approval of others, whereas secure people know they are already approved. They've already taken their seat at the table! Because they don't seek praise, they can give praise. None of us can get honour for ourselves—we can only give honour to others. A secure person does that, and when they do, they see doors open like never before. As a leader, when people thank us for something, we should both receive their thanks ... and give it away.

Do we need people to know what we did? Or are we happy to be an anonymous part of the whole? When I see teams serving, I often wonder, *Am I only hearing about what the team leader has done, or do I know what people in their team have done?* A true leader will always be pointing out the members of their team who are adding great value. It is an indication of insecurity when the need for affirmation rises or when someone has to point out the success of their idea or their hard work. The Bible clearly says, "Let someone else praise you, and not your own mouth" (Proverbs 27:2 NIV). Secure leaders don't give themselves the credit.

4. Secure people can handle failure

By the grace of God, we can all come back from our failures and mistakes. A secure person knows this and understands that Christ always has a tomorrow in mind. Defeat and mistakes are an opportunity to learn how to be better and do better. While insecure people are defensive and unable to handle failure, secure people are open to learning. When we clearly see ourselves as 'jars of clay', we can handle the fact we will make mistakes and be wrong without giving up, giving way, or giving in to depression and despair, self-blame and doubt. As Winston Churchill once said, "Failure is not final, it's the courage to continue that counts."

5. Secure people encourage everyone—not just their own

It is easy for leaders to celebrate those they have raised up, the fruit of their own input. But a secure leader can love and believe in those they have had no part in raising up. Kingdom culture enables us to encourage everyone around us without being territorial or parochial. As leaders, it is not only those we have personally believed in and invested in that we should champion.

6. Secure people inspire others to believe in themselves

When comparing the leadership styles of Hitler and Churchill, Boris Johnson once remarked, "Hitler made you think *he* could do anything. Churchill made you think *you* could do anything." Churchill inspired people to believe they could be the solution, they could be the answer, they could do what was needed.

Secure leaders know that it doesn't all rest on them. We get in the danger zone when we think that we are the answer to every problem. It is a leader's Achilles' heel to think we are better at fixing things than everyone else and never release others to go and do it better. Secure people are often not the hero of the story. They allow someone else to be.

7. Secure people are emotionally stable and at peace

When our soul is secure in Jesus, nothing can interfere with our internal peace. Secure people don't operate out of a need for affection or approval because they know they are loved and accepted. Christ is their rock, their stability, their security.

> *He who dwells in the shelter of the Most High will*
> *rest in the shadow of the Almighty.*
> *Psalm 91:1 NIV*

This was the certainty Jesus carried in His ministry. He suffered rejection, yet it did not hinder His calling or His sense of security. Rejection and accusation are exceptionally painful. It takes time to process life's difficulties and return to a place of confidence. In ministry, John and I have found that the key to persevering is knowing whose approval matters. We may doubt ourselves and question ourselves for a season, but ultimately what keeps us on course is knowing we are secure in God's love. We get to choose to lay aside our insecurities and operate out of a revelation of who we are in Christ and a confidence that our life and times are in God's hands.

Secure in Christ

As leaders, it takes time to grow in our sense of personal security but because we are in Christ, we can operate from a place of security. We can learn to praise others liberally, to be lavish with our compliments and encouragement. We can choose to be kind to ourselves rather than beating ourselves up for our mistakes. We can share our secrets of success, be deliberate about celebrating every person who has a calling on their lives, and release others rather than clinging to our position.

    The greatest gift we give those we lead is our own personal security. We are seated and celebrated. We gain our approval when we look into the face of Christ. We have no need to feed on the crumbs of man's approval when we feast on His. We need to allow God to take us to our seat.

CHAPTER NINE

Who's Carrying the Lunchbox?

One morning I was reading the story of Jesus feeding the five thousand. The crowd was tired and hungry. They'd been following Him everywhere, even into remote areas. Jesus was imparting great teaching, but He was also attuned to the physical needs of those who had gathered. The need was obvious. The crowds were hungry.

Jesus asked the disciples to give them something to eat. "Don't send them away," He effectively says, "You feed them. Set a table for thousands."

When they looked around, there was no food to be found—until they discovered a little boy who offered what he was carrying. He offered what he had brought to the disciples—not knowing that a lunch that was designed to feed just him alone, was about to feed multitudes. He created a legacy with his lunchbox!

Leaders Carry Something to Offer

As leaders, we often think we carry something that's primarily for us—maybe it's our ability to make money or generate finance, our creativity and expression, our time, energy or initiative, any of our talents, our outlook, our attitudes . . . when we give it to God, it has an impact on the lives of many.

Jesus gladly received something that at first looked insignificant. Taking the loaves and the fishes, He said a blessing and broke them, then began distributing them to the crowd. Elisabeth Elliot once remarked, "If my life is broken when given to Jesus, it is because pieces will feed a multitude, while a loaf will satisfy only a little lad."

In one young child's hands was a lunchbox, it contained small fish and loaves, one little lunch. This child had come bringing something, something he had carried and yet at the same time was prepared to give away.

When we come to people, are we carrying something that could help? What could we bring that might cause the miraculous intervention of God in people's lives? Leaders surrender what they carry to Jesus knowing that it has far greater impact than if they had never given it to Him. They are those who are willing to be generous with their time, energy and resources. Each of us has a lunchbox. The lunchbox speaks to us today about caring for the needs of others, sharing what we have, and carrying things we are willing to give away if the Lord asks.

This is an important principle. Leaders are those who are never empty-handed. Sometimes we bring something to offer. Other times we carry something weighty; we are bearers of burdens.

Leaders Carry the Load

In the Old Testament, God's people had to carry the place of worship, the tabernacle, on their backs (Numbers 10:11-21).

The Israelites were living in a non-fixed location, continuously moving from place to place, following God's presence.

> *Sometimes the cloud stayed only from evening
> till morning, and when it lifted in the morning,
> they set out. Whether by day or by night,
> whenever the cloud lifted they set out.*
> Numbers 9:21 NIV

The tabernacle was literally carried by a group of people. They packed it down and carried it on their shoulders. These Israelites were carriers of God's presence, a team. For the whole process to work they had to be unified, they had to keep a sustained pace and maintain a corporate commitment to move when God moved. They had to stay in alignment with one another and with God. They weren't all pulling in different directions—they were together in the goal of ensuring that wherever the people dwelt, God also had a dwelling place.

Just as the Levites carried the tabernacle of the Lord from place to place, we too are to be carriers of His house and His presence. Everyone who serves in the life of the Church and in kingdom purpose is, like these Israelites, a carrier of God's house, His tabernacle, His dwelling among men.

Leaders Share the Load

So often, when leaders are struggling to build and establish something of significance, it is because there is a spirit of independence rather than interdependence. We can go a long way using what we have to achieve what we want, but that doesn't necessarily bring about the greater kingdom purpose. There needs to be an alignment of our gifts with God's blueprint. Your individuality is beautiful and powerful—but for the manifest wisdom of God to be revealed through the church, it needs to come about through everybody serving in a unified way.

Great leaders show people how to align what they carry with God's purpose.

> *His intent was that now, through the church,*
> *the manifold wisdom of God should be made*
> *known to the rulers and authorities in the heavenly*
> *realms, according to his eternal purpose that he*
> *accomplished in Christ Jesus our Lord.*
> *Ephesians 3:10-11 NIV*

Leaders Bear the Weight

The structure of the tabernacle was heavy—the canvas, the bases, the wood, the curtain, the sacred objects—it all needed to be packed down, transported, unpacked ... and it needed to be done whether they felt like it or not, whether they were rested or not.

> *They camped or travelled at the Lord's command.*
> *Numbers 9:23*

Carrying the tabernacle was no easy task. Even the pegs of the tabernacle were made of bronze—they weren't made of light, flimsy material (Exodus 38:20). The bases for the frame of the sanctuary walls and the posts supporting the inner curtain each weighed thirty-four kilograms—and there were a hundred of them! (Exodus 38:27). Carrying the tabernacle required teamwork, strength and endurance. Every Levite needed to be determined and willing to carry weight.

It strikes me that this would have required great humility. Some needed to be willing to go first; others needed to be willing to go last. Each person needed to walk in the same direction as the others and at the same pace as others, so all the parts would arrive together.

A great work for God needs a company of believers who think this way. So many people are willing to expend energy if it benefits themselves, while others focus on guarding their energy and capacity. When everybody plays their part, the wellbeing of everybody is preserved. It's not one at the expense of another.

We can carry more of the load when we're not also trying to carry our own baggage. A leader deals with the things that are weighing them down because they know that they will have a greater capacity to carry what God asks of them if they are not burdened with things that Jesus invites them to leave at the cross. They need to stay light!

It's a paradox of leadership that to carry responsibility and bear one another's burdens, we need to live unburdened. As we choose to carry the cross, we are freed by the cross! The very cross we choose to carry is the cross that lightens our load.

> The only secret sauce in cooking is the one made from passion and hard work.

The tribes of Israel couldn't have carried what God wanted them to carry if their personal baggage was weighing them down. For them it was practical, but for us, the baggage we must not be weighed down by is often spiritual and emotional. Fear, worry, anxiety, unforgiveness, doubt, offence, guilt, sadness, discontent, comparison . . . these are burdens that will weigh us down. When our personal baggage has been released, we have room to be a God-carrier. We have room to be a carrier of faith, potential, dreams, and vision. There is a burden we carry that is not from God, and a burden we can carry that is from God. There is a choice, an exchange of burdens to make—if you will.

Leaders Carry Legacy

The scale of Moses' wilderness tabernacle was extensive. It was designed for a million people to use, and according to many Bible references it was probably in use for five hundred years until Solomon built the temple. What they built in obedience and what they carried on their shoulders ministered to people for hundreds of years. It was an incredible legacy.

As leaders, we all have a part to play.

Like the boy with the lunchbox, we can live generously, with an open hand. The more we give, the easier it is to give. Whatever we offer to the Lord, He multiplies. From what I have seen, the leaders who have the greatest impact tend to have something in common—they are always ready to offer what they carry.

When we choose to bring what we can and do what we can, we create a way for God to turn up in people's lives. We create a way for people to have a greater measure of faith, we inspire their potential, we see their dreams encouraged, and we welcome the presence of God. "Let us not become weary in doing good, for at the proper time we will reap a harvest if we do not give up" (Galatians 6:9 NIV). If we are willing, we may even feed thousands with one lunch.

CHAPTER TEN

The Centre of the Table

Traditionally, the seat at the head of the table has been viewed as the place of honour. But the picture in my mind is something more like what we see in Leonardo da Vinci's painting of the Last Supper.

In *The Last Supper*, da Vinci places Jesus at the centre of the table. The technique he used was called 'one point perspective'—where all the lines in the painting converge in one place, known as the vanishing point. Da Vinci used this strategy to emphasise the importance and central position of Christ. In doing this, he was expressing a foundational tenet of Christian belief: the centrality of Christ.

This is an amazing reality—that God is less hierarchical and more communal. He loves to be found 'in the midst' of His people. The place He is most worthy of is at the Centre of the Table. This is the leader's job: to make sure Jesus is always given His rightful place.

It's easy for leaders to fall into the mindset, especially when things are going great and God is moving, that they are the answer to and solution to every problem, that the success story is all about themselves.

The reality is that leaders do make things happen, they are exciting to be with, and they can solve problems. But the question we must always come back to is this: *Who is at the centre of the table? Who is getting the attention—and the glory?*

Some people say the truest test of a person is not in failure but in success. *Who gets the praise when things go well?* It may be that we are taking the prime seat at the table and we need to move over for Jesus to take His rightful place.

In John 12, a dinner is being served in the home of Mary, Martha and Lazarus in Bethany. At that meal, Jesus is the centre of everyone's focus.

> *Six days before the Passover, Jesus came to Bethany, where Lazarus lived, whom Jesus had raised from the dead. Here* **a dinner was given in Jesus' honour.** *Martha served while Lazarus was among those reclining at the table with him . . . Meanwhile a large crowd of Jews found out that Jesus was there and came,* **not only because of him but also to see Lazarus,** *whom he had raised from the dead.*
> John 12:1-2, 9 NIV

Lazarus was now a celebrity. It would have been so easy to focus on Lazarus. The fact that Lazarus was at the table was a resurrection miracle! But I love that the text simply says that Lazarus was 'among' the others, reclining. Even though Lazarus was a curiosity and might have had things to say about where he had been whilst dead, their attention was on the presence of Jesus.

It would have taken great intentionality on the part of Lazarus to redirect the focus onto Jesus. This is true for every leader. The dinner we serve needs to always be in Jesus' honour. Every good thing happening must be attributed to His presence amongst us.

The phrase 'honour the presence' is not just something we reserve for a church service. This is what we all must do, always, in every part of our lives. Wherever we go, we look for opportunities to position Jesus in that place. How can we bring Christ into the environment we are in? If He is central in our lives, we will innately want to make Him central everywhere we go.

The guests at Bethany made Jesus the most important person at the table. They made it all about Him. The crowd wanted to see both Jesus and Lazarus, but at the table, the attention was on Jesus. It could easily have been all about Lazarus, but it wasn't. Lazarus *was* resurrected. They *could* have focussed on the miracle. Instead, they turned their focus to the miracle-worker!

Even when God uses us to demonstrate His miraculous power, even when we sense His hand on us in unusual ways just as Lazarus had, we need to make sure it is Jesus and not us that is the central focus.

Who Steals the Show?

When we were in New York, it was on my bucket list to see a Broadway show. We let the kids choose, and they picked the hit show 'Aladdin'. When we arrived, the theatre was not what we expected. It was ageing and had slim rows and rickety seats. The fact that real estate costs a premium in New York seemed to take on an even greater meaning when we saw how closely spaced the seats were—when we sat down, we were tightly squashed, with people in front and behind. Finally, the lights dimmed, our anticipation was high, and from that moment on, we weren't even aware of our surroundings! The show began and it had the wow factor! The vibe was electric. What really captivated us though, was the Genie.

Aladdin had been the focus of the show but was superseded in the 'cave of wonders' scene when the Genie hit the stage. The genie's voice was strong and resonant, he was larger than life, his scene got the best special effects, and he used American vernacular to add humour; "Ain't nobody got time for that." His songs, jokes, stage presence and connection with the audience, were spectacular. Whenever the Genie was on stage, nobody was looking at Aladdin. They were fixated on the Genie. When the actors came out for curtain call, guess who got the loudest cheer? It was not Aladdin or Jasmine—it was the Genie. The Genie stole the show!

Ever since Robin Williams reinvigorated the show, making the Genie so attention-grabbing, Aladdin has needed a rename or rebrand. Perhaps 'The Genie of the Lamp' would say it better! That night, there was no doubt about who was the real star of the Broadway show. It was the Genie.

I wonder sometimes if, like the Genie, we have stolen the show, become the title act over Jesus. This can happen so easily without us even knowing, not just as leaders and preachers but in any form of ministry. We all want praise, but sometimes we hog the limelight.

We are here to make it 'all about Jesus'. There is to be no doubt in our minds that *we are here to ensure that Jesus steals the show.* We want to position ourselves so that Jesus can enter our plans and programmes at any moment. We need to lead in such a way that we are never central to what we do. We are to live with Him as our centre.

As Christian leaders, we all start out because of Jesus—He is why we choose to serve and offer our lives, our time, our giftings. It's all about Him ... at the start. But the tension comes when we are in the middle of doing what we are doing. *Does it remain all about Jesus, or has something else filled that spot?*

How does this manifest in our lives? We begin talking a lot about ourselves and don't want to seek to learn and understand from others. We are exhausted because we are trying to do everything ourselves rather than releasing others. Perhaps we don't want to give up our status as 'the expert', so we keep doing things. Rather than taking ownership and responsibility, we begin 'credit hogging'. Or maybe it's not that we have placed ourselves at the centre—perhaps we have simply put the success, the miracles, the results at the centre—just as people were trying to do with Lazarus.

The question we must all ask is: Who are we building people to?

We build people to ourselves when we are at the centre because we like the role we play, but we can get a grandiose view of ourselves, and in doing so, we do not create a secure future for the people we lead. One of the reasons we need to point people to Jesus is so that if anything happens to us, their faith is not shaken. Lazarus, while he was a living miracle, was going to die again! It was no good to have people's faith revolve around Lazarus—they needed to have their faith built on the person of Jesus. Lazarus was resurrected—but Jesus was the Resurrection and the Life!

When People Give Us Undue Honour

King David understood that there is a level of devotion that should not be given to a man but only to God.

> *And David said longingly, "Oh, that someone would give me water to drink from the well of Bethlehem that is by the gate!" Then the three mighty men broke through the camp of the Philistines and drew water out of the well of Bethlehem that was by the gate and carried and brought it to David. But he would not drink of it. He poured it out to the Lord and said, "Far be it from me, O Lord, that I should do this. Shall I drink the blood of the men who went at the risk of their own lives?" Therefore he would not drink it.*
> *2 Samuel 23:15-17 ESV*

The challenge for David was that his men were giving him a place of honour that was beyond what he could accept. They were willing to risk their lives to bring him a glass of water. In response, David passes the honour on to God. He's explaining that that level of honour should not go to him—it was a rich offering of love that could only be given to God.

In his leadership, David realises two things. He valued the service and love of his men *and* he saw that the level of devotion they gave him was only because of the grace of God on his life. David gives the Lord the credit; he gives the Lord the devotion that is shown to him. David doesn't receive it, he points his men back to the Lord. As a shepherd boy, David knew who God was, and when he became a King, he never forgot.

Jesus Gets the Glory

It can be easy as time passes and success comes our way to think that perhaps it's just a little bit about us. But the foundation of our service must remain that it's all about Jesus, it's all for Him. "Why am I trying to write an amazing song?" *To glorify Jesus.* "Why am I running this church?" *To make an environment for the exaltation of King Jesus.* "Why am I building a business and raising finance?" *To generously sow for the purposes of Jesus to be established.* "Why do I do what I do?" *It's **all** for him.*

> *For from him and through him and for him are all things. To him be the glory forever! Amen.*
> Romans 11:36 ESV

The apostle Paul kept Jesus at the forefront of his ministry. He writes: "I worked harder, but it was the grace working with me" (1 Corinthians 15:10). He knew that every success was God's success. He knew it was all about Him. The same is true for us.

It's all from Him.
It's all through Him.
It's all about Him.

His name is more important than my fame (and, thankfully, my infamy as well).

The greatest mark of success for any leader is that we bring people closer to Jesus. It's not that people notice us—what we did, what we said, what we gave—but that in all these things we serve God with our best.

We must desire to do whatever we can, with whatever we have, to make it all about Jesus.

How do we keep it all about Jesus? We remember why we serve in the first place. We do it because He is worthy of our everything.

I pray that as leaders our desire will always be for Jesus to steal the show. We are to be used for the display of His glory. Let's make room for Jesus to show up and show off! Let's willingly move aside so that He can always be found at the centre of the table.

THE LEADER'S TABLE

Main Course!

CHAPTER ELEVEN

Oil on the Table

Every time I visit my nutritionist, she tells me I need to include good fats in my diet. She insists that the best way to ensure I don't forget is to always keep a bottle of oil on the dining table. If it's out of sight, it's out of mind. She knows I need a constant reminder to have oil at every meal. I needed to see the oil on the table as I sat down to eat.

As leaders we need to follow the same advice—we need constant access to fresh oil if we are to have an effective ministry.

The same was true for Jesus. He is our pattern and our model. This is why it is so important when we pursue leadership or ministry, that we first seek the anointing. Jesus did nothing to advance the kingdom until He first received the anointing!

To the people of the day, this was unexpected. They were looking for a Messiah—someone who would take the kingdom by force—but God's will was that the kingdom be advanced, not by might or by flesh, but by the Spirit of God.

Jesus was extremely clear that the anointing of the Spirit was the source of His ministry. His first words ever spoken publicly were a direct quote from the book of Isaiah:

> *"The Spirit of the Lord is upon me, for **he has anointed me** to bring Good News to the poor. He has sent me to proclaim that captives will be released, that the blind will see, that the oppressed will be set free, and that the time of the Lord's favor has come."*
> Luke 4:18-19

Both the Old Testament and the New Testament confirm that the anointing that rested on Jesus was the Holy Spirit.

> *God anointed Jesus of Nazareth with the Holy Ghost and with power.*
> Acts 10:38 KJV

With the anointing, we can do what we could never do by the flesh.

It's the difference between natural and supernatural ministry. It's the ministry of the Spirit that sets people free. As leaders, we need the anointing that 'breaks the yoke'.

> *In that day his burden shall be taken away from off your shoulder, and his yoke from off your neck; and the* **yoke shall be destroyed because of the anointing oil.**
> Isaiah 10:27 MEV

The yoke signifies slavery. This could be physical, spiritual or emotional—anything that stops us from living the life God would have for us. Whatever the bondage, the anointing can break it! It's the oil of the Spirit that allows us to cut through every natural limitation and every demonic assignment or curse. As leaders, our ultimate ministry in the Holy Spirit is that God's children would be no longer slaves but would walk in the glorious freedom that belongs to them.

Jesus is called Christ (Greek, *chrīstós*), meaning "anointed one". Christians, therefore, are 'anointed ones', just as the name suggests. To be a Christian is to be anointed with grace and gifts by the Holy Spirit. It's no surprise that everything that is opposed to the kingdom of God is seen as 'anti-Christ'—it is anti the anointing!

The devil is happy to see powerless believers operating in leadership—men and women who have all the best intentions but no real power to bring breakthrough and spiritual transformation. Everyone can bear fruit, but not everyone has a life that breaks through the darkness, sets people free, and results in lasting spiritual impact.

Being anointed enables us to do the work God has called us to do. Not just to merely do it, but to make a difference. We can do good work for God—but *anointed* work can achieve something intangible, something that has the touch of God on it. As those who minister, we need to know when the anointing is there and when it is not. It is spiritually discerned, and while it is hard to define, it leads to great effectiveness and great impact.

Keep the Oil Close

When we come to Christ, we all receive an anointing. As believers, we have already been given oil. 1 John 2:20 (NIV) says, "But you have an anointing from the Holy One, and all of you know the truth."

As a leader, you can access the anointing you have already been given as a believer! It's there on your table, ready to be used. Every time we stand on a platform, every time we lead a life group, every time we invest in the lives of others, we need to reach for the anointing oil. Not only that, we need to reach for a plentiful supply. When we are dripping with the anointing, it's going to leave a mark. Everywhere we go and with every step we take, we will leave behind oily footprints, a holy residue.

In the Old Testament, the anointing oil was used on specific occasions and by specific people. When people were anointed, the oil was poured on their head, their garments, their hands and their feet. This anointing set them apart, consecrating them to the Lord and making them holy. The use of oil was to establish priestly and kingly authority. This oil for kings and priests was not dabbed on, it was not a drop—it was liberally poured over them.

When we come to the New Testament, the oil flows even more liberally! In Christ, we have all been made kings and priests unto God (Revelation 5:10). We all have the anointing!

How Anointing Works

The anointing we have received from the Holy Spirit is sometimes referred to as 'unction.' Unction is what moves us, teaches us. It is an inner understanding, an intuitive following of the Holy Spirit's lead. Unction enables us to lean into something we haven't necessarily thought through but we know has originated from God.

Jesus flowed with unction. We see this in the story of the woman at the well. Jewish travellers avoided the route through Samaria, but Jesus knew He needed to go there (John 4:4). Jesus knew that in Samaria there was a divine appointment waiting for Him. The disciples were shocked when they returned to the well and found Him talking to this woman. Jesus was doing something He wouldn't normally do because He was flowing with unction. This became a pivotal encounter in Jesus' ministry as He declared for the first time that He was the Messiah. He also positioned Himself, not just as the *Jewish* Messiah but as *everybody's* Messiah! Jesus ended up staying two days in the village where the Samaritan woman lived, and many in the village believed in Him. The unction led to a phenomenal milestone in His ministry.

When Jesus encountered a paralysed man lowered from a roof, the unction led Him to not deal with the obvious 'seen' issues first. He saw what was unseen. Everyone else thought that the paralytic needed to walk. But Jesus knew what the real issue was that weighed heavily on this man's heart; He could see the greatest sadness in the man's life . . . and it wasn't his external condition. Led by unction, Jesus could see that the biggest issue—the yoke that needed to be broken—was the sin that was ensnaring his soul. Jesus knew what needed to be addressed first; He knew the right order in which to minister effectively. The anointing directed His ministry. Jesus ministered to the paralytic man's internal condition first, and perhaps this is what made his external healing possible.

When it comes to leadership, God will choose those who operate in the anointing over those who do not. He looks for it in every expression of service. Something like working in construction or feeding people at tables might seem like quite ordinary activities, but even in these ordinary outworkings of service, God is looking for those who work with anointing.

In Exodus 31, Bezalel and Oholiab are noted as men with great skill *and* with the anointing. They are chosen to work on constructing the tabernacle because they are not just talented, they are anointed. Serving God requires more than our skills and our talents—it requires the anointing. God is not impressed by our talents if they don't carry His touch.

Your skillset becomes supercharged when you have the anointing!

The early apostles knew the importance of the anointing for those who served God. In delegating some of their daily duties, they gave instructions to the believers to find and choose people who were full of the Holy Spirit, not just those with wisdom or good administration skills. These skills would surely have been enough to do the job, but they insisted that people were picked because they carried the Spirit. These people weren't just setting up tables, they were laying a table. They needed the Spirit of God to do the work of God.

Are we trying to work without the anointing? It will all be so much harder. If we want things to flow smoothly, we need the oil. Oil removes friction and creates free-flowing ease. If there is a lack of anointing in a leader, this impacts their teams—if there is a lot of friction, there's probably not a lot of oil.

As leaders, not only do we need a liberal supply of oil, we need fresh oil. We need a fresh anointing. Unlike wine, oil does not get better with age. High-quality oil always comes with an expiry date on the bottle. The truth is, really good oil is fresh oil. We must keep our oil supply fresh. But there is a price to pay for fresh oil. It takes waiting on the Lord, immersing ourselves daily in His presence, keeping ourselves ready and waiting for Him to turn up. It takes an investment of ourselves. We must take time to pray and seek God to receive it, to pay the price to keep the oil flowing and fresh.

Waiting on the Lord is essential to the anointing. Jesus wants to dine with us, not have us go through a drive-through for a quick top-up. Oil, just like perfume, rubs off, wears off, and fades away over time. Let's make sure there is always fresh oil on our table.

The ease, effectiveness and impact of our life and leadership require the anointing oil. Don't try to lead without the anointing.

CHAPTER TWELVE

Anointed at the Table

Interestingly, in addition to His baptism, Jesus received three distinct anointings and they all took place at dinner parties. This is quite surprising, but it suggests that for us as leaders there may be anointings that will only be unlocked as we sit around a table.

The first dinner-time anointing is found in Luke 7 at the house of Simon the Pharisee. While the meal is already underway, a 'sinful woman' comes into the room, kneels before Jesus, washes His feet with her tears and wipes them with her hair, kisses His feet, and finally anoints His feet with rare perfume.

This is one year into Jesus' ministry and two years before Jesus is going to be crucified. Jesus' response is to say to this woman, "I tell you, her sins—and they are many—have been forgiven" (Luke 7:47).

Because she had been forgiven much, she loved much. Her coming and anointing His feet was an expression of her love and thanksgiving towards Jesus. She understands He is her redeemer. She has seen the power of sin being broken. In many ways, this public anointing of Jesus' feet was symbolic of the office Jesus had as Priest, the one who could cover and forgive sins. Her public anointing showed Jesus' ability to break the power of guilt, sin and shame.

Jesus' second anointing was around a table in the house of Lazarus, Mary and Martha at Bethany. It was six days before Passover, and Jesus knew that the cross was getting closer. In John 12:1-3 (ESV) we read:

> Jesus came to Bethany, where Lazarus was, whom Jesus had raised from the dead. So they gave a dinner for him there. Martha served, and Lazarus was one of those reclining with him at the table. Mary therefore took a pound of expensive ointment made from pure nard, and anointed the feet of Jesus and wiped his feet with her hair. The house was filled with the fragrance of the perfume.

Like the sinful woman, Mary anoints Jesus, pouring a rare and costly perfume on His feet. During dinner, she comes with gratitude and thanksgiving for what Jesus has done and for who He has been to her and her family—the one who overcame the grave. She has seen Him revealed as the resurrection and the life. Many had questioned previously, "Are you Elijah?" since Elijah the prophet had raised people from the dead and Jesus evidently carried this same resurrection power. I see this act of worship as Mary anointing Jesus in His office as Prophet. Mary knew that just as Elijah had defeated death, Jesus could do the same. She has seen the power of death being broken.

The third anointing of Jesus at a table is in the home of Simon the leper in Bethany, where an unnamed woman broke an alabaster box, anointing His head with perfume (Mark 14:3-9; Matthew 26:6-13). This anointing was a preparation for what lay ahead. In just a few days, Jesus would be crucified. I believe that by pouring the oil on His head, this woman was anointing Jesus in the office as King. He was about to be rejected for being the King of the Jews, but in this anointing, she acknowledges Him as the rightful and coming King, the one worthy of our most costly devotion. It was a foreshadowing of the day when all dominion would be restored to Jesus, a day when every knee will bow and every tongue confess that He is Lord.

After Jesus died, there was no time before the Sabbath to anoint His body for traditional burial. When the women went back to the tomb three days later to complete His burial preparation, they found He had already been resurrected, His body was gone. Jesus was never anointed in death—instead, He was anointed at the table by this unnamed woman before He went to the cross. He was only anointed while He was alive.

This anointing oil that had been poured on Jesus' head so close to His crucifixion would have been retained in His pores. The very moment the crown of thorns, designed to mock His kingship, was pushed into His head, the fragrance of that anointing would have been released into the atmosphere. While being publicly reviled, Jesus had a fragrant remembrance of His public confirmation as King of kings. The anointing spoke truth to the lie.

In His most horrific experience, Jesus had a constant reminder of who He really was and what He had come to do. What an amazing thought that because of this anointing, our Saviour was literally the fragrance of life among those who were perishing. It's significant to think that in the midst of His suffering, Jesus was reminded of who He was doing it for.

Around a dinner table, Jesus was anointed for His role as priest, prophet and king. He would conquer sin and death, and dominion would be His.

If Jesus was anointed around tables, what does it mean for us? These public table anointings are prophetic. When we receive a public anointing, it can push us to our destiny and endorse our future. They are a public 'appointing', a recognition from those close to us of the authority God has conferred on us. Confirming what God wants of us and that He has His hand on us can come through the words and actions of those around us.

I'm sure, for Jesus, these three anointings were a beautiful endorsement and encouragement, a sign of love and devotion. These women worshipped Him and ensured He knew why He was doing what He was doing. It was a reminder for Him of why He needed to go through what lay ahead.

There is a prophetic push to our destiny when we receive this kind of anointing.

These anointings of Jesus showed that He was being received by the people, embraced by the people, needed by the people, and that He was the solution for the people. These anointings revealed that He had a mission to complete and positioned Him publicly for what He was about to do. He had already been chosen by God. Now He had been endorsed by people.

The anointings Jesus received were a preparation, an endorsement, and an encouragement. Jesus had the most significant calling of any of us and had already been anointed by His Father, yet He highly valued the anointing of those around Him.

Anointings do not happen in isolation.

We must stay connected to people if we are to receive the public anointing we need for the ministry God has appointed us to.

As a leader, I have anointed people at tables. I have asked people to step up, recognised talents and callings, prophesied, prayed over and anointed people with oil. There is a fragrance God wants to place on His ministers that comes from the hands of the people around them. The fellowship of believers is powerful to lead us into all that God has for us.

Why was Jesus anointed at tables? These anointings Jesus received came to Him because He was serving the people who anointed Him. His love and impartation into their lives was what led them to these acts. We can't as leaders expect anointings if we don't accept burdens.

What does this mean for us as leaders? I believe our calling and ministry are to be acknowledged and unlocked in the company of others and not only on our knees in prayer. As we connect with people, what God has placed in us is revealed. A public anointing takes what God has done in private and seats us in our ministry office, propelling us into our destiny.

CHAPTER THIRTEEN

Freedom is on the Menu

"Today's special is a healthy serving of freedom."

Imagine if people rolled up to your house and this was the sign on your menu board. As leaders, our ability to lead people into freedom is a crucial reason why we have the title 'leader'.

Jesus came to heal the broken-hearted, to set the captives free, to release those who were oppressed. He came to forgive *and* to deliver us. He came to restore our sight *and* to pour out His favour. He wants us, His disciples, to bring not just salvation, but freedom, to His people. Everything that He did, we can do!

As leaders, we need to be confident to minister freedom to others. We minister to the whole person—body, soul and spirit. If people are to experience the overflowing, abundant life of God, we need to make sure that freedom is always on the menu.

One way we bring freedom is through the ministry of deliverance. When I was in church in the nineties, the demons were running scared—we were binding and loosing and lifting off demonic oppression left right and centre! Unfortunately, deliverance and freedom ministry since then has often been seen in a bad light. The world has done its best to depict deliverance as something negative, something it is not. But when we flow with the Holy Spirit and with love for the people, deliverance brings glorious freedom.

I'll never forget the night that I received deliverance from a couple of spirits that had a hold on me. The most remarkable thing was the physical 'lightness' I felt afterwards. The sense of being weighed down and tightly bound that I had experienced for a couple of years was completely gone. My old patterns of thinking still needed to be renewed, but I wasn't restricted any more—I was free!

In Matthew 17:14-18, we read:

> *A man came and knelt before Jesus and said, "Lord, have mercy on my son. He has seizures and suffers terribly. He often falls into the fire or into the water. So I brought him to your disciples, but they couldn't **heal him.**"*
> *Jesus said, "You faithless and corrupt people! How long must I be with you? How long must I put up with you? Bring the boy here to me." Then **Jesus rebuked the demon** in the boy, and it left him. From that moment **the boy was well.***

I love that the words healing and deliverance are interchangeable. Being delivered is being healed, being healed is being delivered.

Jesus has just had a very special personal moment. He has been up on the mountain with Peter, James and John where He has been transfigured and Moses and Elijah have appeared and talked to him. God the Father has again affirmed audibly that Jesus is His Son with whom He is pleased. It's a precious, transcendent moment. On coming down the mountain once again, Jesus is immediately brought back down to earth with a thud.

A large crowd is waiting for Him, there's an anxious father, and the disciples haven't been able to help his demon-possessed son. Jesus doesn't mince words—He's not very pleased that His disciples couldn't take care of this without Him.

The father expected that the disciples would be able to heal his son.

Jesus expected them to be able to do it.

They should have been able to do it.

So why were they unable to help? Why couldn't they bring the change and transformation that was needed? Jesus tells them they have a faith problem. In verses 19-20, we read:

> *Afterward the disciples asked Jesus privately, "Why couldn't we cast out that demon?" "You don't have enough faith," Jesus told them. "I tell you the truth, if you had faith even as small as a mustard seed, you could say to this mountain, 'Move from here to there,' and it would move. Nothing would be impossible."*

Faith was the key to freedom, to healing, to help. The minute Jesus prayed for the boy, he was well. Jesus was full of faith. The faith we need is a certainty in the power of God; it is the knowledge that God wants to see His people freed. It is the belief that if we ask for something according to God's will in Jesus' name, it will be done.

If Jesus came to set the captives free *and* promised us that in His name we would do even greater things than He did, why would we doubt our mandate and authority to pray and see things change? We are here to command the demons to submit to the authority of Christ, to pray for physical healing, and to believe for deep-seated traumas and abuse to no longer torment individuals.

This is what I stand on when I pray: that God in His grace does good things for His people, that Jesus' death and resurrection allow us to minister in the power of His blood, and that it is God's will for His children to have victory in every area of their lives. The other thing I stand on is the belief that persistent prayer changes things and that Jesus encouraged us to ask, to pray, *and* to believe. If things can't be changed through prayer, He wouldn't have said that they can.

As a leader, we must ultimately carry a revelation of the cross. This is foundational to ministering with authority. So often, we create environments that offer warmth and connection, love and concern, inclusion and friendship—and all these things are very important. But as Christian leaders, we must offer something more. Our goal is not just to draw a crowd or grow our circle. The demon-possessed boy was surrounded by a well-meaning group of people, but there was no change for him, no freedom. We must be able to see and discern where there is need and bring faith to that situation.

Not everyone needs deliverance, but everyone will have situations in their lives where they require pastoral support. Jesus expects us to be able to help. Spiritual oppression can be internal or external, and as leaders, we can deal with both. Never doubt that you are able to help!

Can you see why someone is stagnated in their Christian maturity? Can you see what is holding someone back from stepping into their calling? Can you see what could change and do you have the faith that God can do it? We need to be those who, knowing the power of the blood, pray with authority and see the forces of darkness destroyed.

As leaders, we have a heart for people to grow, mature and be blessed, and we have a duty and a responsibility to see them set free. We need to go beyond offering entry-level Christian grace and offer next-level Christian faith.

Are you frustrated with someone who seems to be stuck in the same problem week after week? Have you actually helped them, or just sympathised? Let's not be holy sympathisers but holy believers. Empathy, mercy and compassion are vital if we want to get the surgical gloves on and dig deep into people's lives, but exhortation, encouragement, prayer, deliverance and words of wisdom are also vital to send that problem packing. We need a culture of acceptance and grace, but this needs to go hand-in-hand with a culture of empowerment and faith. Nothing is impossible for the one who believes!

There are people who can't get free on their own. We are the ones who see the need and bring the solution. So what do we need to do to be able to help?

Firstly we must be empathetic. Many of Jesus' miracles took place because He understood what the person was experiencing. He had compassion for people's situations and struggles. When people are tormented or bound, we must not be dismissive or stand in judgment. Love must be our first response. Our actions and words must flow from love for God and each other. Love brings down walls and allows for honesty.

Secondly, we must be ready to minister. Ministry is not something we can always plan for. Jesus was always ready for whatever He faced. He was continuously filled with the Spirit. He was aware of the prompting of the Spirit. As ministers, being 'already ready' is essential. We can't afford to be without Bible verses to declare or a personal overflow to minister from. The Word of God is living and active, but as Oswald Chambers said, we need to keep the Word of God always living and active *in us*.

Keys to Ministering Freedom

Freedom is sometimes more than just a moment of deliverance. There are three key considerations we must think about when we minister to people.

1. What can the person handle?

The Pharisees were put down by Jesus because they made the burden of do's and don'ts incredibly complex and hard. We need to be careful not to overburden people with what we ask of them. When Jesus ministered life change to the adulterous woman, He simply said to her, "Go and sin no more" (John 8:11). He didn't give her a 'six steps to wholeness' programme, nor was there a lecture. The truth is, she already knew what she had done. Jesus simply empowered her with the freedom and permission of a new beginning, a fresh start. Faith is about making things possible, not hard, not impossible. We need to understand that by helping people take simple steps forward, eventually, the problem that seemed so massive will be behind them.

2. What does the person want?

As leaders, we want people to go to the next level in their faith or freedom but we need to be careful not to rush them. Jesus' whole ministry was to usher in the kingdom, but Jesus didn't explain the parables to everyone who heard them. Jesus was always seeking to draw His disciples to the next level of faith, but He only invited Peter to step onto the water. In fact, Peter was the only disciple who even considered doing it. We need to be careful not to push people where they are not ready to go, or they will feel discouraged and like they are failing. We can at times see potential for greater levels of freedom for a person but we often need to wait until they are ready.

People have to want to be free. It's common for people to 'make friends with their demons' and be unwilling to see them for what they are. I have found that it is much better to minister to those who want and ask for freedom than to those who need me to tell them they need freedom. The times I have done that have not been very successful. It's just quite awkward. You can lead a horse to water, but you can't make it drink. Freedom must be something a person wants, something they get thirsty for. We may be wasting our efforts if freedom is not what they want or are asking for, and we risk making people feel afraid and unsettled.

3. How will we activate the person's faith?

A key realisation as leaders is that we are the faith-activators. Many times, we have to activate a person's faith for them to receive freedom. We can do this by sharing our testimony, speaking words of encouragement, and declaring verses that remind them that as believers we all have spiritual authority. We can help faith rise through praying, prophesying, or giving a 'rhema' word, something God is saying specifically to them. As leaders, we must flow in the gifts of the Holy Spirit as we minister.

If I am going to bring someone into a place of freedom, I often ask them to name the problem, to own it. Then we pray, breaking the chains that bind them, declaring the blood of Jesus over them, and if needed, helping people come to a place of repentance and confession. They may also need to be led in a declaration about their freedom and identity, thereby affirming the Lordship of Christ in their lives.

> No one is born a great cook. One learns by doing.
> – Julia Child

When we have prayed for someone, we need to make sure we cement a certainty in them that this is something that can't be lost. We are shoring up the freedom they have received. Jesus has done a finished work, and the freedom they have received is also a finished work. We confirm the new level of freedom they now have by speaking encouragement and hope into their future.

～

Jesus' entire desire was to set captives free. He wants all of His children to experience the glorious freedom that belongs to them. When we minister in His name, we can be sure that heaven is cheering us on. Let's not doubt God's great power that is at work in us. He has given us all authority in heaven and on earth.

Luke 10:19 tells us that we have full authority to overcome the power of the enemy—every demon in hell, every darkness, every problem, every sickness, every challenge, everything we face in life. Greater is He that is in us than He who is in the world (1 John 4:4).

God is looking for leaders who will face the darkness head-on. Let's not just serve up care and concern. Let's serve people with Spirit-empowered ministry that sets them free.

Freedom is not just on the menu, it's the speciality of the house!

CHAPTER FOURTEEN

A Leader Worth Their Salt

In Roman times, a *salarium* (salary) was a sum of money given to soldiers which they could use to purchase salt and other essential and valuable items. There is some debate as to whether the soldiers were actually paid in rations of salt which they could then trade for other items, or if they used their *salarium* to make their own purchases of salt. Either way, the idiom "worth one's salt" was coined. In Roman times, people were often referred to as 'being worth their salt'—or not.

As leaders, to 'be worth our salt' is to be deserving of respect because of our integrity.

When we start out in leadership, this is perhaps our greatest challenge. People want to know, can you be trusted? All leaders must have integrity because integrity is vital for trust. Why should anyone put their trust in us if we do not walk with integrity?

When John and I moved cities to start a church, we were completely unknown. We could not move our reputation with us, social media wasn't prevalent like it is today, Facebook didn't exist, nor did X or Instagram. We'd had a vibrant ministry in Auckland for seven years, but we couldn't build on that reputation in our new city. We were on our own. The only things we had were a call from God, our savings ... and our integrity.

To lay a foundation of trust, people needed to see that we were true to our word. Right from the start, we made sure that whatever we said to people, we could do. It would be no good to espouse grand ideologies if we couldn't faithfully do the small things we had promised week-to-week. We were always aware of the leadership maxim, "under-promise and over-deliver". This is because it speaks directly to a leader's integrity. If a leader makes a promise or says something will be done, their integrity, their leadership capital, is now tied to this. If they do what they have promised, people will trust and continue to serve the vision. However, if the leader fails to deliver, people quickly lose trust and the vision can be compromised before it gets off the ground.

Fair enough, really. People often make considerable sacrifices to partner with a visionary leader, and it's not easy when we don't follow through on our word. If we say we're going to give out five hundred packs of hot cross buns, we do it! Integrity means we don't put out a vision that we have no intention or plan to follow through on. (Of course, there are times when mitigating factors cause delays or changes, and in those times, it is crucial that the leader communicates what's happening so that trust is sustained.)

Are we keeping our word and following through on what we said? Are we communicating transparently any change of course or plans so those we are leading know what's happening? Our personal integrity undergirds our leadership integrity. God isn't wanting us to lead as a politician, selling a dream but not delivering.

A Person of Integrity

A person of integrity is the same person no matter where they are—in public or in private. David knew the importance of this. In Psalm 101:2 he writes:

> *I will be careful to live a blameless life ... I will*
> *lead a life of integrity in my own home.*

This is at the core of what a person of integrity looks like. There is no separation between their public life and their private life. They are not one person in one setting and someone different in another. This person cultivates wholeness of heart and singleness of mind. They do not 'play act' in public—they are the same at all times. Isn't that a refreshing thought?! I love the fact that as leaders, we are not called to be performers on a stage but to live authentically both in and out of the spotlight.

Integrity in the Life of David

King David was a man who lived wholeheartedly for God, and for most of his life, even before he became king, he lived with great integrity. On one occasion, during sheep-shearing time, David and his men were camped near the home of a wealthy landowner called Nabal. While they were there, David and his men were very good to the household of Nabal. David protected Nabal's entire household from marauders and thieves—in fact, all the time David was there, no harm came to Nabal or his property.

Knowing it was a time of celebration and plenty, David asked Nabal to share food and provisions with him as compensation for what he had done. When he learned that Nabal had screamed insults at the messengers who had asked on David's behalf and refused to give him anything, David readied his men to fight. Nabal had wronged David by not providing him with food. Understandably, David was angry.

Abigail, Nabal's wife, heard about what had happened and hurried to give David wise counsel, advising David to avoid bloodshed and murder. She emphasised that he would have a 'staggering burden' on his conscience if he killed innocent people. We find Abigail's words in 1 Samuel 25:28-31:

The Lord will surely reward you with a lasting dynasty, for you are fighting the Lord's battles. And you have not done wrong throughout your entire life ... When the Lord has done all he promised and has made you leader of Israel, don't let this be a blemish on your record. Then your conscience won't have to bear the staggering burden of needless bloodshed and vengeance.

Rather than give in to his emotions, David chose to walk in integrity. Instead of reacting rashly, he listened to Abigail and changed his course of action. He accepted Abigail's gifts and left vengeance in the hands of the Lord. Amazingly, he didn't have to wait too long before the Lord vindicated his cause. Nabal died soon after from a stroke.

David had been let down by Nabal. His work was undervalued, and his expectations of gratitude were unmet. However, David's response, in the end, was mature. David trusted in God to outwork justice. If he had not done this, maybe his kingship would have been in jeopardy. David could easily have been just another Saul. Instead, his actions flowing from his integrity led to his blessing and promotion.

Interestingly, Abigail is also promoted. When her awful 'fool of a husband' dies, she gets a new one: David! (Sounds like she got the ultimate upgrade!) She becomes the wife of the future king. Because of her integrity, David recognises her worth and she too is promoted to a position where she has standing and influence. Integrity bears fruit!

1. Integrity lets us rest easy

David had no anxiety because he knew he had acted rightly. His conscience was burden-free. When we live a consistent life, we too have nothing to fear and nothing to hide.

*Whoever walks in integrity walks securely, but
whoever takes crooked paths will be found out.*
Proverbs 10:9 NIV

Until that time, David had always gone to war for a reason. Now, when he was faced with personal provocation from Nabal, would he respond with violence? David chose to let it go. As a result, David was able to rest easy.

An astute French proverb says, "There is no pillow so soft as a clear conscience," meaning that if there is nothing to worry the mind or to hide from others, sleep comes easily.

I once stayed in a bougie hotel with a pillow menu. All kinds of different pillows could be ordered with just a phone call to a concierge. I was stumped—there were more than nine different options on the menu! I stuck with what I had and I slept just fine. But I'm afraid that sometimes, what keeps us awake isn't the type of pillow we use. *Is there something God is asking us to do that we have been ignoring?* Sometimes, what keeps us awake is what's weighing on our conscience! What we need most of all is the easy sleep of one who has a clear mind and heart.

2. Integrity creates stability

David's integrity allowed him to make a reasoned and logical response. He chose to listen to advice rather than to react from his emotions. When we don't allow our emotions to lead us, we are more even-keeled and more reliable as leaders.

Early in my ministry, I made a decision that my emotional state would never impact my leadership interactions. I didn't want people to wonder, *Which Gillian will we meet with today?* or *Which Gillian will I face today?* I wanted them to be sure that they would meet someone who was consistently gracious, calm and measured. I might have had concerns or things weighing on my mind, but I determined that my personality was going to be even-keeled. No one needed to worry that they were going to get 'angry Gillian' or 'snappy Gillian' on any given day.

As leaders, we must not let our emotional world overflow into the lives of others. People need leaders who exemplify stability. I remember what it was like working in retail for unstable bosses. Every morning I woke with a sense of dread. What mood would they be in? It was a very stressful way to live, and made working with them full of fear. I had to summon my courage every time I went to work.

One of the keys to our effectiveness is that we don't let emotional responses guide our leadership. Emotionally stable leaders empower emotional stability for those around them. It's easier to trust a leader who is predictable than one who swings to extremes in mood or behaviour. People learn that they can trust that leader's judgement.

A person of integrity is consistent and constant and therefore inspires trust. People will not feel confident to share their heart and soul with us if they cannot trust us. But when people trust us, unity forms, hearts are aligned, and so much more can be achieved.

Responding like David

What do we do as leaders if people have let us down, not met our expectations, or undervalued us? We have to put disappointment and hurt in God's hands and leave it with Him. We have to trust God. We must pursue integrity as a core value of who we are. Our character is everything. It's what makes us worth our salt.

David allowed his responses to be questioned. We need to ask questions of ourselves and each other: *Are we building our lives on the Word of God? Are we dealing with small issues in our lives before they become big issues? Is there any part of our life we wouldn't want others to know about? Are we more interested in character than reputation?*

Who we really are is more important than who people think we are. I've always been struck by the fact that our reputation does not always correlate with the reality of who we are. Jesus said to the church in Sardis, "I know your deeds; you have a reputation of being alive but you are dead" (Revelation 3:1).

Twenty years into leading our church, John and I went through a season where our integrity was publicly and rather vehemently questioned. It was an awful time for us, but through it all, we were reminded of the opposition Jesus faced and how He responded to it.

The Bible tells of many people who encountered accusations and judgement even though they were people of great integrity. This was often their moment of greatest testing. Would they continue to forgive? Would they choose to not hold onto offences but to bless those who were cursing them? Would they allow the demotion, humiliation and accusation they faced to change their desire to love, forgive, and serve the purposes of their Heavenly Father? Their response in the face of opposition testified to their integrity.

The hard times we go through may not always be deserved, but they are always a test of our integrity. God is looking for leaders He can trust—leaders who are truly 'worth their salt'. Will we continue to love and bless

> Kitchens are hard environments and they form incredibly strong characters.
> – Gordon Ramsey

and serve, despite what others do to us or say about us? As leaders, we must determine that we will maintain our devotion to the ways of Christ, come what may. We may lose friendships, we may lose everything we have worked to build, but if we hold to our integrity, we can never lose what is most important. The reality is, integrity costs us something, but it is always worth it.

Let's make it our goal as leaders to continually grow in integrity. As we listen to the still small voice of the Lord, we will rest easy, build trust, and create an atmosphere of stability for those around us. This is what mature leadership looks like.

CHAPTER FIFTEEN

Waiting on Tables

At the Last Supper, perhaps the most important meal of all, Jesus showed the future leaders of the church the nature of the leadership they were to embody.

> *"If I then, your Lord and Teacher, have washed your feet, you also ought to wash one another's feet. For I have given you an example, that you also should do just as I have done to you."*
> John 13:14-15 ESV

In washing their feet, Jesus was showing His twelve disciples the style of kingdom leadership they should aspire to. When Jesus bent down and washed their feet, it was an act of love. He wasn't just concerned about their dusty feet. He was symbolically showing them that they were clean spiritually as well. He was demonstrating concern for their whole person. And, He was modelling servanthood.

What was the nature of that servanthood? It wasn't just that He took the menial jobs. In His actions, Jesus was meeting both the spiritual and physical needs of the disciples in that moment. It was a beautiful expression of His willingness to serve them in every way they needed.

When Jesus stooped to wash their feet, He was making sure His disciples were prepared both physically and spiritually for what would come next. With clean feet, they were ready to sit at the table that night. With sanctified hearts, they were able to serve alongside Him in the work of the kingdom.

One thing John and I have always done as leaders is send flowers to people at significant moments of their lives. It is only a physical gift, but it conveys our love for them and our heart for them. We wanted to minister to their whole person—letting them know we see them, that we know what they are going through, and that they are valued in this moment. We want to *show* them that our hearts are with them. When we pair something that is in our heart with a tangible expression, it reaches people's spirits. They never forget what the action conveyed.

Sometimes, we need to take our message to its most basic form in order to touch hearts. This is what Jesus was doing. To get His message across, He needed to get down on His hands and knees. He loved the disciples intimately, and He was willing to lay aside His position of honour in that environment to minister to them.

> *Jesus, knowing that the Father had given all things into His hands, and that He had come from God and was going to God, rose from supper and laid aside His garments, took a towel and girded Himself. After that, He poured water into a basin and began to wash the disciples' feet.*
> John 13:3-5 NKJV

Jesus could lay aside His garment and take this menial task knowing it didn't change anything about who He was. He knew the Father had put everything in His hands and that taking the place of a servant did not in any way affect His leadership or the greatness of who He was. His greatness was not fundamentally expressed in the most revered tasks—it was about doing what was needed in each situation. Jesus was displaying the character of the Godhead, showing us that love and service are inseparable.

Because we know our calling, we are able to meet others' needs at a cost to ourselves, with no sense that it diminishes our leadership. Leaders take the initiative, even if the job feels 'beneath them'. Jesus was modelling to the future leaders of the church that they were to serve the needs of people in the same way—with disregard for their own position, pride, or personal comfort.

At the Last Supper, Jesus didn't just teach His disciples—He modelled to them the principle that they were servant-leaders, not positional leaders. Through His example of serving them, He showed them how to lead. Just as He was about to literally lay down His life at Calvary, He was showing them that their leadership would involve laying down their lives day after day. To lead with humility, we must be so secure in who we are that we can prefer others over ourselves.

I'll never forget driving with my kids in the car to church when they were very young and still figuring out their place in the world. "We're a pastor family," one of them said, "... and that means we are the boss of the church!" We had deliberately included our kids in the mission of building the church—we were doing this as a family, and they understood they had a part to play—but I quickly addressed this with my own instruction. It was one of those sacred parenting moments. "No, darlings," I gently corrected them. "We are not the boss of the church. Being the leader means we are the greatest servant of the church. Whatever the church needs, we do our best to meet that need." It was a profound moment in the car as the truth of that statement hung in the air. I wanted them to understand, "Don't take the lead unless you're actually willing to be last, not first."

When Jesus was finishing His training of the twelve and setting them up to have kingdom authority, they had to understand this same principle. The authority they had was primarily about a willingness to serve, to benefit others. Their leadership was primarily based, not on what they knew or their gifts or talents, but on their willingness to wait on tables. Jesus had given them a picture that painted a thousand words. He was showing them the greatest way to love and lead people.

We know that the disciples learned this lesson because in Acts 6:2-4 we see that the apostles were *literally* waiting on tables! It's a beautiful display of their heart to serve that they understood that no task was 'beneath them'. Great leaders are always willing to 'don an apron' and serve others.

The apostles were meeting the needs of people through feeding them. But, like Jesus, their service was not expressed in only one shape or form. As the church's needs grew, the nature of their service also changed and grew. It soon became apparent that the greatest way these apostles could serve the emerging church was by delegating some duties and focusing on the spiritual needs of the people. They were to hand over one role to serve in another.

My friend Leanne, a noble and godly leader who I greatly admire, modelled this extravagantly to me one evening. It was an Easter Sunday, and Leanne and her husband had preached and led at multiple services across the weekend. They had also hosted John and me in their home for the past two weeks. If anyone needed a break that evening, it was Leanne. Instead, she invited twenty of their campus pastors over for dinner. She recognised that these leaders had worked hard all weekend and also were in need of refreshment. Instead of asking them to bring food or help out in the kitchen, she prepared a meal, set the table, and created a space for them to relax and laugh and spend time in fellowship.

I knew Leanne when she was a youth pastor and it was amazing to see that, in the midst of an ever-increasing ministry and co-leading a church of thousands, her heart to serve hadn't changed. In spite of her own burdens and vast pressures, she continued to serve her leaders. This didn't diminish her own leadership position—it strengthened her leadership.

Jesus could have asked someone else to do the foot washing that day, but instead, He did it Himself. In serving others, there is no diminishing of who we are. In fact, this is what makes a leader truly great—that we are always willing to 'wait on tables'.

CHAPTER SIXTEEN

Serve the Right Food

Leaders give people the food their hearts crave, the food of encouragement. Encouragement is what makes our world and the people in it grow. Our leadership, our marriage, our kids will all thrive when we include the key ingredient of encouragement. Encouragement makes a hearty meal! Leaders know the power of the words they speak to build people and build the church. They serve up lots and lots of encouragement.

The Holy Spirit shows us the incredible power of encouragement to bring growth and multiplication. In Acts 9:31 we read:

> *The church had peace ... and it became stronger as the believers lived in the fear of the Lord, and* **with the encouragement of the Holy Spirit, it also grew in numbers.**

A spirit of encouragement, when present, causes the church to grow.

What does this spirit look like? And, more importantly, how can we embody it? Paul talked a lot in his letters about encouragement being the goal of his visits to the different locations he travelled to.

By the will of God I will come to you with a joyful heart and
we will be an encouragement to each other.
Romans 15:32

When we get together **I want to encourage you in your faith.**
Romans 1:12

Paul was liberal in his use of encouragement. He used it to build faith and strengthen the believers, as well as to inspire and breathe life into the church.

Paul valued encouragement in all its forms. He loved both to give it and receive it. Paul was facing hardships and conflicts in every direction. Yet when Titus arrived, he brought great encouragement:

> *When we arrived in Macedonia, there was no rest for us. We faced conflict from every direction, with battles on the outside and fear on the inside. But God,* **who encourages those who are discouraged,** *encouraged us by the arrival of Titus. His presence was a joy, but so was the news he brought of the encouragement he received from you. When he told us how much you long to see me, and how sorry you are for what happened, and how loyal you are to me, I was filled with joy!*
> 2 Corinthians 7:5-7

Encouragement is a culture that we create. It is life-giving, and it always comes full circle. The sowing and reaping principle applies beautifully with encouragement. Paul had already visited the believers to encourage them, and now they are encouraging him! When we choose to sow encouragement, we also end up reaping a harvest of encouragement.

As leaders, we need to intentionally cultivate the practice of encouragement. We do this primarily through the words we speak. Our words carry the power to lift people and bring momentum and growth in their lives.

SERVE THE RIGHT FOOD

The words of the godly encourage many.
Proverbs 10:21

Let everything you say be good and helpful so that your words will be an encouragement to those who hear them.
Ephesians 4:29

The reality is, many people need encouragement because they struggle to believe in themselves. In his article, *Be a Belief Magnet,* John Maxwell writes:

> "The ultimate transfer of a leader . . . is when leaders take the belief that they have for their people and pass it on until the people own it. It's not borrowed. The first way to help other people believe in themselves is to actually believe in them."

We must not miss the people who are right in front of us. Everyone needs encouragement. It forms resolve. It sets direction. It builds their confidence—both in themselves and in the part they are called to play in the greater vision. It's an expression of love—love that sees the best in people and hopes the best for them. It enables people to do more than they thought they could. It's a way of loaning people our confidence.

Encouragers are consummate believers in people.

The apostle Paul knew the value of encouragement. He wrote, "Encourage each other . . . build each other up" (1 Thessalonians 5:11, 2 Corinthians 13:11).

For a while, I engaged the services of a personal trainer. There's no way I would have ever worked as hard or produced the same results on my own. My personal trainer's belief and encouragement strengthened my resolve to work as hard as I could and to become as strong as I could. On my own, I would have felt a bit lost and I certainly wouldn't have pushed myself to my limits.

His motivation made me want to turn up, commit to improving, and keep at it until I saw the results.

Encouragement connects us with the very best version of ourselves. The world tends to put us in our place. People quickly equate confidence with arrogance. Instead of championing each other and cheering each other on, the world is quick to mock, put down, or criticise. Criticism is the opposite of encouragement. Criticism deflates, encouragement elevates.

I have a friend who grew up with a father who never once encouraged him but always told him how he could have done better and what to improve on. There was no doubt he loved his son, but in his desire for him to be the best he could be, he robbed his son of the fatherly affirmation he needed. This father never fully celebrated his son's achievements or made his son feel that what he did had value. With such an 'encouragement deficit', it took a conscious decision for this man to act in the opposite spirit. Yet today he is one of the most encouraging people I have ever met. Because he grew up without encouragement, he knows the power of it and wants to make sure people receive what he was never given. He is now a great leader of a healthy, growing, and beautiful organisation—a man who is first and foremost known and celebrated for his spirit of encouragement. His natural environment could easily have left him feeling inadequate, but he saw the vital importance of starting a new legacy in his family and circle of influence.

Encouragement is particularly important for those serving in ministry or in a public-facing role. When others are looking on, the pressure is on. People are influenced by the level of enthusiasm and energy we bring. In the words of Tozer, "God dwells in a perpetual state of enthusiasm." God never has a bad day! For us to maintain our passion, we need encouragement. It's the fuel that keeps us energised.

Battling self-doubt and discouragement is common for many ministers. It can be so easy to believe in others, and at times, so much harder to believe in ourselves. Ministry requires us to be unusually vulnerable. Ministry leaders don't get to hide—they put themselves on display for all to see. Their weaknesses are amplified when they stand in front of a crowd. They are under pressure to be full of fresh revelation and have fresh oil.

We need to be deliberate about strengthening and encouraging those we are developing as leaders as they step up in ministry. We all need to be encouraged to keep going, even if we still have more to learn. Encouragement draws people out and it draws their gifts out. People are confident and happy to be shaped in their ministry gifting when they are being built up at the same time.

As a leader, we need to hear from God and meet the needs in the room, but it is easy to get it wrong when we have a microphone in our hands, adrenaline pumping, and a congregation hanging on our words. I have a performing arts background—I am familiar with a well-rehearsed and 'pitch-perfect' delivery. Ministry that is authentic tends to be anything but rehearsed! When God starts moving, anything can happen, and leaders need the confidence to be spontaneous, to flow with the Holy Spirit, and to courageously step out of the boat. When people get to minister in an environment of encouragement, it's easier for them to 'find their feet' in ministry. Encouragement helped me move from a mindset of needing to get everything 'just right' to being free to take risks in my public ministry.

It is still a scary thing to share a word of knowledge, not knowing if someone is going to respond. I have seen many miracles of healing and deliverance in those moments, but there have also been times when no one responded. That is hard! *Maybe I heard wrong?* We all second-guess ourselves and we all fear rejection, but in an environment of encouragement, we know we cannot fail.

One of the first times my husband, John, preached in a large, influential church, he was astounded by the environment. Person after person who took the platform displayed incredible talent. There was so much gifting in the room! John couldn't understand it—until it was time for him to preach his message.

When he was finished, he came down from the platform feeling like he'd done a really bad job. But after the service, one person after another came up to him and told him how amazing the message was and how much it spoke to them. John noticed how people did the same thing to those who were on the dance team . . . and the worship team. In that moment, he realised it was not that there was more talent in that church, but that the talent and confidence of the people were flourishing because of the encouragement they received.

Encouragement in Our Teams

A lack of encouragement creates coldness in our teams. People are driven to become more competitive as they vie for the crumbs of encouragement, whereas encouragement will produce warmth and connectedness. A lack of encouragement can also cause people to act self-important because no one else is showing them that they are important.

Some people use flattery instead of encouragement to build people up—but it doesn't work. Flattery is about wanting people to like us. It builds people into needing us, whereas encouragement is about propelling them into a ministry function that doesn't need us. People are not sustained by honeyed words that do not nourish or strengthen. Leaders who are immature use flattery to manipulate. Ultimately flattery is not for the person it is given to—it is self-serving. As leaders, we don't serve up flattery—we serve up encouragement.

So how do we cultivate a spirit of encouragement? If we are lacking in a spirit of encouragement, we need to find it first in God. We must deliberately seek and receive the encouragement of the Holy Spirit for ourselves. He is the encourager, the one who builds us up. When we receive this from Him, it is easy to give it to others. It becomes the natural overflow of God's Spirit in our lives.

An Encouragement-Rich Environment

The way we create an encouragement-rich environment is by making our encouragement specific, deliberate and liberal.

Encouragement needs to be specific. The more general or vague our words are, the less impact they have. We don't just want to say, "Good job." Instead, we need to tell people exactly what they did well, what they did that was truly great. When we give details and mention examples, our encouragement gets right to the heart and touches people deeply.

Encouragement needs to be deliberate. We need to be intentional about looking for opportunities to encourage people. Take the time to identify what is special about who they are and what they are doing. Choose to focus on the good, not the improvements they should make. Leaders look for and create opportunities to be an encouragement. Have the attitude of, *I'm going to go out of my way to find a way to encourage you!* Paul wrote letters to emerging leaders—we can text and email leaders. It's a special thing when someone makes a deliberate effort to communicate encouragement.

Encouragement needs to be liberal. We may have said it before, but we need to say it again and again. People will never tire of being told they are awesome at something. Repetition does not diminish the value of our words. People need to hear something more than once to believe it. Remember, we want to be *belief magnets*. Our belief in people needs to be so strong and sustained that they eventually believe in themselves.

∼

As leaders, let's make it our goal to have a paradigm of great encouragement. We don't want to limit people's development by thinking too small about who they could be. We need to see the bigness of the possibilities God has for them.

They may be destined to do more, become more, and achieve more than we can ever imagine. Learn to see *big* for people!

Leaders have the potential to be the most encouraging people on earth. Some of us may need to stop serving up sarcasm, criticism, or mockery. Our words carry weight, so we must stop and think before we speak. The tongue can start a fire that is not easily put out. Remember, very few people have an ego that tells them every day that they are amazing. All of us need to be acknowledged for the good things we do, our success and our wins. So, speak with kindness. Tell people what's special about them. Notice what people do well—and tell them!

Jesus was aware of the power of His words. In John 6:63, He says, "The words I speak are spirit and they are life." When we choose to keep the spirit of encouragement in our words, we breathe life, health and growth into those we lead. Like the apostle Paul, let's be leaders who are always seeking to encourage others. Encouragement is the greatest food a leader can serve.

CHAPTER SEVENTEEN

Try New Recipes. Innovate.

My son's favourite meal is spaghetti bolognese. I have cooked countless spaghetti bolognese meals over the years, and he has always loved it.

One of the elements that makes spaghetti bolognese really good is the garlic. Using garlic to its best effect is difficult. I tried many times to figure out how best to add it—I chopped it into little pieces, I grated it, I pressed it with a knife, I sliced it—I tried everything to get the perfect garlic flavour but it never seemed like I got it quite right. It was either too strong, or there were big clumps of garlic in the dish, or it barely made an impact. I even tried ready-made garlic in a tube. That was hideous. Then finally, like an answered prayer, I discovered a life-changing device: the garlic crusher! All that's needed is to peel a clove, put it in the crusher, turn the handle and *voila!* Garlic pops out with the perfect consistency—*and* the flavour is perfect! When I used the garlic crusher for the first time, my family enthused that it was the best bolognese I had ever made, the flavour was so superior! Amazing how one little tweak brought such a big change. My bolognese is better now than it's ever been!

Sometimes in life, a little tweak can bring a big change. A fresh thought, one little adjustment, and the most awesome things become possible. All it takes is one innovation. Great restaurants have their staple favourites, but they also change the menu at strategic times to keep things fresh and interesting. Are we willing to keep creating, to keep trying new things, to 'change the menu', to 'alter the recipes' in our leadership?

As leaders, we can easily become set in our ways and lose the enthusiasm to change. But change is inevitable—we can't avoid it. Leaders who embrace change and proactively lead their organisation are able to stay on the cutting edge and retain their effectiveness throughout their tenure. Those who innovate are the ones who see God do amazing things!

William Booth, the founder of the Salvation Army, used contemporary pub songs, rewriting them with Christian lyrics and 'modernising' the church experience to reach many people. When George Whitefield, an eighteenth-century preacher, was barred by the Church of England from preaching in their pulpits, he took to the open air to preach and was instrumental in bringing about an incredible revival known as the Great Awakening. These two men took obstacles and barriers to the gospel and found a way to overcome them. They imagined new ways to do things and were hugely impactful for the expansion of God's kingdom.

It is so easy for the methods we have always used to become traditions. We have to watch out for this because traditions can soon become entrenched as religion. Religion opposes innovation. Religion wants to do things the way they have always been done. Religion maintains the rules; it allows things to become stale because it fails to embrace what God is saying or doing *now*. Religion starts when we cling to our life experiences or the habits we have developed. These can be our greatest obstacles to innovation.

When God wants to do new things, He requires humility from us. Others may not understand why we think change is important or why we need to do something new. As leaders, humility allows us to stay flexible, to be willing to behave differently and think differently, and even be willing to look stupid.

We have to accept that what once worked might not always work. Our tried-and-true way of doing things may stop working. It's so easy to defend what we have always done, but we need to change with the times. We need to see the day we are in and see what is most effective now. We can keep things feeling new and fresh when we remain willing to innovate no matter how many years into our story we are.

Strategic Risks

Queen Esther is a great example of someone who came up with a new strategy to bring about God's will on earth. During her time, the Jewish people were facing the threat of extermination. King Xerxes had signed a decree that they could be attacked, killed, and have their property stolen. Essentially, he had signed a death certificate for all the Jews in his kingdom. Esther was encouraged by her uncle Mordecai that, as the queen, she could be uniquely enabled by God to help her people. "Perhaps God has placed you there for such a time as this," he reminded her. Even so, she didn't know what to do or how to change the situation.

So what did Esther do? She prayed and fasted for three days, and during that time she received a God-breathed strategy. She prayed and she innovated. She found a way to get the king's ear, to make him hear her heart and see her problem. Even though it was against convention, she entered the king's throne room. When he asked her what it was that she wanted, she didn't present her request straight away. Rather than throwing out demands, she threw a dinner party. She set a table, to turn the tables. She invited King Xerxes and the enemy of her people, Haman.

When the king came to her banquet, he asked her again, "What do you want?" Instead of answering his question, Esther invited him back for a second meal. She took a delicate approach, she was careful to 'set the table' so it would lead to a favourable outcome. Esther was waiting for a sign that the prayer and fasting had shifted things—and she was intentionally building distrust between the king and Haman. In her invitation to the first banquet, she clearly stated the occasion was for the king. Haman was merely an add-on to the guest list. In her invitation to the second banquet, she made Haman seem equal to the king by saying that the banquet was for both of them. Perhaps she knew that by arousing the king's jealousy he would be quicker to turn on Haman when she presented her plea.

The sign from heaven Esther was waiting on came just before the second banquet. King Xerxes had a sleepless night. Opening the scrolls, he remembered that Mordecai had never been honoured for saving the king's life. The next day, Haman was charged with parading Mordecai around the city in the sight of all the people. Esther could see that Mordecai was being honoured and Haman was being humiliated.

Because of this, Esther was now sure that God was working on behalf of His people. So at the second dinner party, she finally presented her people's plight to the king. She was leaning into her creativity and innovation, but she was also very aware of the leading of heaven. Heaven loves to partner with our risk-taking!

Esther was in a desperate situation. Her people had no way out, their futures were on the line. In their despair, they began to seek God—and in turn, they received an incredible game-changing innovative plan. God gave Esther a new way to do what she needed to do and because of this, she was able to convince the king to modify his decree and empower the Jewish people to turn the tables on their enemies. It took grit and courage, but Esther accomplished God's purpose.

God's innovative whisper is often closest when we feel the most desperate. The hardest moments we face often require the greatest changes. Sometimes when we feel like things are at their worst, God is ready to do great things. We just need to be prepared to try something new, however risky it seems.

A Fresh Approach

In the midst of what's difficult, we need to pause, look for God, and begin to think outside the box. We may stop, we may falter, we may even feel unworthy. Maybe all we can see is our lack and inability. But we must see Him. He is the author of innovation. Don't give up. If God has asked you to do it, there is a way! Sometimes it only takes one idea, one new thought, one new revelation, for things to turn around. The Bible is full of examples of people who trusted God to do new things and as a result, experienced breakthroughs and miracles. God has a fresh approach for new victories.

I remember asking God for a strategy for our women's ministry. As a church, we were running in-person women's events twice a year in each of our major campuses. These were held at night, and women absolutely loved them!

> Chefs don't make mistakes, they make new dishes.
> – Lizzy Smith

But for our volunteers, this was another event in an already full calendar. As a leadership team, we decided to simplify and prioritise our activities and our energy to ensure what we were doing was sustainable for both our staff and volunteers. We put everything we were doing on a whiteboard, and one by one, we crossed out events, including the one I was most passionate about—our regional women's nights. I began asking God how I could disciple the women without these events. Until then, this had been our primary tool for speaking into the lives of our women.

I was driving along one day when God showed me an unexpected strategy. He gave me the idea of filming four sessions every year and creating a curriculum based on the key topics I wanted to disciple the women in. These video sessions could be used in all of our women's small groups around the country. This strategy had so many surprising benefits. Not only did it lighten the load for our staff and volunteers, but there was a multiplication of impact that I never foresaw. Now the women didn't just hear one message—they heard multiple messages that all built on one another and took them deeper in their faith.

I was amazed at God's strategy. Our small groups could choose to re-watch these videos, and new groups could pick them up and watch them even years down the track. With my time freed up, I was able to minister more widely, and soon people from other churches began using the same curriculum. When we embrace change, we can often find it is a stepping stone to greater things!

As leaders, the need for change comes at many different junctures. We can choose to see change as difficult and frustrating, which it certainly can be, or we can decide that change is vital if we are to remain current and fresh.

In leadership, as in the kitchen, fresh is always best. *Is there anything in your life that feels stale or overcooked? Are there ways you are doing things that are not working?* It's time to innovate, to re-create, to dream again, to look at our situations in a new light. Let's be leaders who pray and ask, seeking out new methods and enjoying the greater impact God has for us.

CHAPTER EIGHTEEN

Dine Together, Dream Together

The lamp lights are on, the night dims, and everyone huddles around the table, the odd abandoned plate disregarded as the warmth of camaraderie makes this holy gathering feel like something you never want to leave. Something is unfolding here that you've been longing for. You've carried a vision, you've seen it by faith—but now those nearest and dearest to you are catching it too. It's on nights like these, when we linger around the table, that some of the most significant, most inspired leadership dreams take hold. For some, this will be the moment they discover what they've been longing for. As you share, they begin to realise there is a plan . . . a part to play . . . a dream that won't be as good without them.

A Shared Vision

I often think that John and I must have the noisiest home in the neighbourhood—always cramming as many people as possible around the table! Much of the way we lead comes through the joy of talking about what is on our hearts when we gather at the table. A dream from God is a worthy thing to share, but it remains a dormant seed until we open up and let people in.

To outwork a magnificent dream, we need a team, and we need a team who can see it and who can help shape it. The best teams are those that dream together. Great unity arises from dreaming with your leaders. I believe that vision and unity are inseparable.

I love that Jesus shared His vision and His future plans with the disciples. He didn't keep the details close to His chest. He told the disciples what His purpose was—to suffer and die. He also wanted them to be aware that they were part of His plan for the redemption of all humanity. Like Jesus, if we can dream with others, we can change the world. Leaders unify people around a shared vision.

A Clear Vision

One of the most important things we do in leadership is communicate vision. People need a vision to rally to. It is often said that the absence of vision leads to division. When people unify around a shared vision, they achieve more than they could as individuals on their own. We are being built together as living stones (1 Peter 2:4). With Jesus as our chief cornerstone, our interdependence allows us to build something greater.

Is your team clear about what the vision is? Do they know the kingdom purpose they are trying to achieve? As leaders who want to align people to vision, we need to be able to see it clearly in our minds before we can articulate it clearly. If the leader has clarity, the team will also have clarity.

Clear vision comes through faith. Faith is vision. It is seeing beyond the here and now. Vision lives in the future, seeing what could be. Vision always expands on the present reality. It takes us from our present state to our future possibilities.

A Big Vision

People are drawn to a big vision, a vision that comes from big faith and big hearts. Vision does amazing things for your team. It:

- Creates energy
- Brings focus
- Feeds passion
- Generates enthusiasm
- Inspires service
- Unifies and aligns hearts

Vision is the fruit of faith and the best friend of momentum. The more people who come together to outwork a vision, the harder it is for one individual to 'stir the pot', creating disunity or lack of momentum.

The right vision always brings life. Proverbs 29:18 (KJV) says, "Where there is no vision, the people perish." Conversely, where there *is* vision people cannot help but come alive!

For a vision to gain momentum, it must be worthy of people's time and effort. People need to see daily progress as well as how it all fits into what is to come—progress for today and a promise for tomorrow.

As leaders, we must take time to talk through vision. It needs to be digested. It needs to be chewed on. It must be able to be 'taste-tested' by your key people. *Do they believe in this vision, this direction? Do they think something is missing?* If your team believes in the dream and the direction, the vision will become contagious.

We can effectively share our vision by:

- Connecting it to where people live.
- Making the vision tangible and practical.

- Declaring vision again and again. It can't be shared too much.
- Prophesying your vision. Speak it out with faith and boldness.
- Helping people visualise the vision. Tell stories that paint a picture.
- Seeing everything as an opportunity to share vision. There are always opportunities to share vision. Don't miss any of them!

What vision are you carrying? How can you make the vision clear? Take a moment and write down what you see. If it is alive in your heart, it will flow out of your mouth. See the most audacious and impossible things God could do through you and your team, and remember . . . God wants to do more than we can imagine!

As leaders, we need to see the vision clearly, believe it passionately, pursue it resolutely, and most of all, we need to share it with others.

CHAPTER NINETEEN

Making Room at the Table

One of the amazing things about a thriving leadership environment is that it attracts new leaders. While this is a huge blessing, it also creates a challenge. As leaders, how do we make room within our existing teams for gifted individuals who may already be established in leadership? These people are used to leadership, they've already got runs on the board. They're used to making decisions, taking the initiative, having authority, and being entrusted with significant responsibility.

A reality of leadership is that other leaders will always turn up. Then, we have a crucial decision to make. Just because these new people weren't raised at our table, because they haven't arrived with our DNA, will we exclude them because of this or will we make the effort to include them?

As leaders, we always find it easier to include those we know, people we are comfortable around, people we have shared our lives with and built memories with. While these people who have journeyed long with us are highly valued and precious, they cannot be afforded the only place settings at the table. Our table must always have room for new people who turn up in our world with gifts, talents and callings—even when they don't come with the same DNA.

Whenever something begins to flourish, it tends to attract more gifted or charismatic leaders into the mix. This makes sense. High-capacity people aren't attracted to low-performing environments. But the reality is, these people are potentially the hardest to include and integrate. How we respond when they come into our world is a test of our leadership.

∼

In church leadership, John and I were very skilled at raising up leaders from within and working with people who we knew well. Because many of them had come to Christ in our church, they were in every way, 'sons and daughters of the house'. It was natural for us to make a pathway for them into leadership. But we also saw the need to be more intentional about embracing leaders who had transplanted into our sphere with gifts and talents that were already defined. Would we use them and adopt them into our world, or would we mistrust them and leave them 'on the outer' simply because we were not the ones who had raised them up and grown their giftings?

I believe that it is critical in our churches and in our leadership spheres that we become an 'adopter'. We can tend to favour those who we have put time into, those whose shaping has been at our table, but if we are going to see true strength in our environments, we need to learn to adopt those we haven't had a part in shaping.

As leaders, we need to embody and value in our churches and our leadership the spirit of adoption. We have been adopted by God into His family and we are to adopt others into ours.

> *God decided in advance to adopt us into his*
> *own family by bringing us to himself through*
> *Jesus Christ. This is what he wanted to do and*
> *it gave him great pleasure.*
> *Ephesians 1:5*

I love this verse! It's in the very nature of God to bring us in. He adopts us without hesitation, and it gives Him great pleasure. We must have this same attitude to others: an openness, a heart to grow our circle of inclusion, a willingness to expand who we trust and entrust leadership to.

What's taking place for people who move into our environment? Their circumstances have changed, they are dealing with being uprooted and replanted, they are adapting to an environment where things may be new and unfamiliar. Do we judge them in that season and measure them by the cultural behaviours we expect, or are we willing to look past different ways of doing things to the heart they carry? They may not immediately understand 'how things are done around here', but that does not mean we should exclude them. Remember, they have chosen to turn up in your world. They have chosen to journey with you, to partner with your vision. They have chosen to belong to your family—but they need to be adopted in.

> Friends buy you food. Best friends eat your food.
> – Anonymous

It's easy to think we do this already, that we include new people, that we're welcoming. But this is about more than being nice and inclusive. Adoption means we *belong* together, not just that we like having them among us as a guest. Adoption looks like, "I believe in you, I choose you, I will enable you to be a part of the vision."

Often these people don't look like they 'need' adopting. They can seem like confident, complete, self-made people who don't particularly need us to provide a platform or a place for their giftings. Because of this, we can tend to leave them to themselves—or worse, not acknowledge or celebrate them. But if God has added them to our world, if He has transplanted them, it's for a reason. Perhaps He knows they can be more fruitful here with us than they were in their previous location.

Are we playing to our favourites, or are we operating with a spirit of adoption? God doesn't have favourites. In Acts 10:34 Paul states, "I see very clearly that God shows no favouritism." When we 'play favourites' we can end up going with who we know rather than who may be best. Often, who we know is who we trust. Trust is earned, but we have to give opportunities for trust to be earned.

Rahab the harlot is a key person who was 'adopted' by the leaders of God's people and went on to play a significant role in His kingdom purposes. She belonged to the enemy nation—the Canaanites—that the Israelites were going to destroy. When two Israelite spies came to study the land ahead of attacking it, Rahab used her talents of craftiness and coquettishness to protect them from being discovered. Rahab recognised that the Lord is God, and she wanted to defect from her people. The spies and the Israelites honoured her for what she did. They brought her into their camp—and into their lives. They received her as their own. She was adopted into the nation of Israel.

Rahab went on to marry a distinguished Israelite from the tribe of Judah. Eventually, she gives birth to a son called Boaz. Boaz marries Ruth. Ruth gives birth to Obed. Obed is the father of Jesse. Jesse is the father of King David, and King David is in the lineage of Jesus Christ. This is incredible!

Rahab the harlot is prized and valued. Her inclusion among the Israelites and into the genealogy of Jesus symbolises the spirit of adoption at work through Christ the Redeemer. She isn't simply acknowledged out of a sense of duty or hosted as a guest—she is welcomed and woven into the tapestry of grace. She gets to be an intrinsic part of the story.

By all accounts, Rahab shouldn't have been adopted. She was the 'wrong' race and culture, she was a loose woman, she was a liar... yet she was adopted because she chose to side with the people of God.

We learn a lot about adoption from the story of Rahab. Firstly, adoption is a two-way street. People have to want to embrace your leadership for adoption to work. There needs to be a reciprocity. Rahab backed up her words with actions. Before the army attacked, she did what the spies had asked her to do. She hung a scarlet rope from her window, she showed her willingness to help them, she took a risk for them. The spies, in turn, had to trust that Rahab would do what she said and not let them down—they had to trust she would not leave them out in the cold. For adoption to work, it requires taking people at their word.

Adoption involves us as leaders having a discerning heart, not a judgmental attitude. The spies could not have known that Rahab would end up being mentioned in the 'faith hall of fame' in Hebrews 11, but they were certainly able to recognise that God had appointed her to be a pivotal part of their future.

Not everyone who enters our world will 'fit the mould', but as leaders, we need to be willing to adopt people generously and with open hearts. I know of situations where people failed to facilitate others because they didn't fit the usual model. These were super-talented people who had demanding careers but were more than willing to play a part, yet because they couldn't attend practices at the prescribed time or attend meetings when the rest of the team could, the leaders saw it as a lack of commitment and decided not to involve them. Talented people often don't fit the mould but we need to realise that doesn't mean they are not on board. We need to find ways to make sure they are included and able to contribute. We need to make sure they feel like they are home.

Are you a pastor? Can you adopt people who are already ministers? Do you feel insecure working with people who come into your world ready-made or fully developed? Do you feel like it's too hard to integrate people because they have 'the wrong culture'? Culture is imprinted on others through proximity, not through distance. For people to belong, they need to know that you like them, that you will listen to them, and that you can see and celebrate their gifts and talents. Culture is caught, not taught. It takes time for people to pick up culture, but their 'sameness' is not necessarily what matters. Variety is the spice of life, and leaders understand that culture can be enriched by the new flavours people bring.

Our willingness and ability to adopt people will ultimately determine how vibrant our environment will become. Remember, the person we adopt might be just the person God has strategically positioned to bring breakthrough to our lives and our ministries. All around us, people are waiting to be adopted. Is there someone you need to welcome to your leadership table?

CHAPTER TWENTY

Uncork the Bottle

Every leader will encounter times when they face a major personal crisis or challenge. By now you will probably have realised that you don't get to checkout of your responsibilities when things aren't great—you have to keep leading. Unfortunately, we don't stop being a leader when we go through tough times personally.

When the pressure builds up, when our life has been shaken up like a bottle of carbonated soda, we need to deal with what we face before that bottle bursts. It is crucial as a leader that we learn how to deal with personal challenges if we are to avoid a leadership blow-up. In our season of pain, it's important that we don't explode. We have to find a way to lead, even while we are feeling the pressure. We need to learn how to 'uncork the bottle'.

John and I refer to our tenth year of pastoring a church as 'our year from hell'. In early February of that year, we broke ground on a multi-million-dollar building project. Exactly one week later, John was out cycling when he was hit by a car. I remember the call: "Don't worry, but your husband's in an ambulance on his way to hospital." When I arrived at the hospital, John was in a neck brace, covered in blood, being prepped for an MRI. One look at him, and I was deeply concerned. There was no telling how bad this was going to be. Straight away, I rang someone from our church's oversight to get his counsel. We needed to come up with a plan in case John ended up out of action. The MRI showed he had fractured his skull. He also had a bad concussion, two broken ribs, and a broken thumb. It wasn't the worst it could be, but it wasn't good either.

The following week, with no warning, I was taken out as well. John was still recovering at home when I was suddenly hit with excruciating pain in my jaw. I collapsed onto the floor in agony. The doctor referred me to a neurosurgeon for further tests. Was it a tumour? John was in la-la-land—deeply concerned for me, but in a floaty sort of way! In the meantime, I was struggling to talk or even smile. Any movement in my face triggered stabbing pain. I couldn't bear to interact with anyone. I couldn't touch my face or brush my teeth. I couldn't eat. When the doctor finally gave me the diagnosis, it wasn't good. It wasn't a tumour, but it was one of the most painful conditions people have to live with. I had no choice but to take a step back from leading the church. I knew I needed to take time off work, but at that point, I had no idea if I would ever have a normal life again.

Not only were we dealing with this, but our whole staff team seemed to be under spiritual attack in that season. For the first time ever, we were leading a team that felt depressed and dispirited and were fighting battles of their own. It seemed like everything was stacked against us. We were in a rough situation. We were leading, but we could feel the pressure building.

In the book of Samuel, we read of a time when David was having one of the worst experiences of his life. He had just returned home from battling the Philistines to find his village, Ziklag, pillaged and burnt to the ground. The Amalekites had come and taken all the livestock and all the women and children. Even David's two wives had been taken.

David was completely distraught, as were all the men who were with him. These battle-hardened, muscle-bound warriors were bitterly weeping and crushed in spirit. Their families were gone.

> *When David and his men saw the ruins and realized what had happened to their families, they wept until they could weep no more. David's two wives, Ahinoam from Jezreel and Abigail, the widow of Nabal from Carmel, were among those captured.*
> 1 Samuel 30:3-6

David had made a massive error of judgment: he had left his home unprotected. When he returns, he knows he's made a mistake, and he's devastated. The men he leads are so angry they are talking of stoning him. Now David's life is in danger. But David doesn't give up. We read "But David found strength in the Lord his God" (v. 6). Even though his men are voicing murderous thoughts towards him behind his back, he doesn't let it take him out. David doesn't run in the face of criticism. Instead, he finds a way to deal with his biggest challenge—the challenge to lead despite his pain.

It's hard to lead or minister when 'the sheen has come off'. As leaders, we can't let our pain determine our actions. In the middle of his greatest crisis, David did not act like everyone else acted. He did the only thing he could—he found strength in the Lord his God. David 'uncorked the bottle'—he vented his feelings and his desperation to the Lord alone.

This is the only way to respond to crisis. We need to learn how to find our strength in God, exchanging our weakness for His strength. How did David manage to deal with the pressure and pain? He did it by reminding himself of past victories, leaning into the presence of God, and choosing revelation over reaction.

Past victories strengthen us for today's crisis. As leaders, every battle we have fought and won gives us the capacity to face difficult days. David had fought many battles before this—both external and internal. He had fought the lion and the bear, rejection and injustice. He had been in tough times before and he had seen God's hand with him. He had already learned to trust God. He knew God would help him.

Strength is found in praise and worship. In his greatest moment of pain, David did what he'd already learned. He knew how to encourage himself through praise and worship. He was primarily a man of worship. He also knew the scriptures—he recited them, he'd memorised them. He remembered what God had done in the past. The faith he already had in God brought him comfort. While others were falling apart around him, he remained emotionally stable.

We need to respond to crisis from a place of revelation. David's ability to stem his internal bleeding, to not allow grief to overtake him and to keep trusting in God meant that he didn't react to the situation. Instead, he responded from revelation. 1 Samuel 30:7-8 says:

> Then he said to Abiathar the priest, "Bring me the ephod!" So Abiathar brought it. Then David asked the Lord, "Should I chase after this band of raiders? Will I catch them?" And the Lord told him, "Yes, go after them. You will surely recover everything that was taken from you!"

David doesn't rush to solutions on his terms. Incredibly, he asks God's permission to go and get his family back. He doesn't take matters into his own hands or default to what he wants in the moment. David recognises that his problems are the Lord's concern, and he asks Him what he should do. God tells him to go and pursue the Amalekites, and He reassures David that he and his men will get their families back.

As leaders, it's so easy to fall into the trap of becoming reactionary when things are going wrong. It's often so much faster to take matters into our own hands and attempt to fix things our own way. But when we do this, we run the risk of making one bad decision after another. It's easy when things are going badly to lose our self-control and go into a frenzy. There's a reason for the saying, "fools rush in". It is crucial to seek God's wisdom rather than react in times of crisis.

David responds with self-control. He chooses to seek revelation. This is a crucial moment for David. Because he has received a promise from God, he can lead from a place of confidence, knowing that God will do what He has promised. Because of revelation, David can set a new direction, turn the men's attitude around, and rally the troops. He can inspire confidence back into the hearts of the men he leads because he has found his confidence in God. David has downloaded courage from God and can now give it to his men. The same is true for us. If we carry it, we can give it! Wise leaders can not only stem the pain in their own lives but are also able to stem the pain in others.

David and his men chased after the Amalekites, and finally, they had success! They had victory! 1 Samuel 30:18-19 (NIV) tells us they "recovered everything the Amalekites had taken . . . nothing was missing." They not only recovered everything that was taken, they also plundered the enemy. When we lead from a place of trust in God, even when we are in pain, the result of our trust is a victory that is even greater than we thought possible. David's men received their families back and were overjoyed.

In our year from hell, after sitting at home and not doing anything for weeks, feeling down and alone, I knew my attitude needed to change. I couldn't attend my church, I couldn't smile, I could barely talk, I couldn't hang out with people. I had to make a choice. Was I going to let the pain take me out? I needed to remind myself that there is always purpose in our pain. God will expand our capacity through difficult times if we will let Him. As leaders, we must choose not to waste our pain. In fact, often our greatest ministries come out of our deepest hurts.

As a church, we were advancing and taking new ground at the time. No wonder we were facing spiritual opposition! In that moment, I made a decision to rise up and fight. I would pay a painful price for every word I spoke, but I had to fill my mouth with true confessions, sow seeds of healing, and declare what was possible in my future. I needed to get back on the front foot of faith.

Even though physically we weren't doing great, John and I decided we would go ahead with our plans to attend a conference in Australia. We knew we needed to be in an atmosphere of faith and breakthrough. At that conference, I could only attend one meeting a day, but I was determined to find my strength in God. During one of the meetings, I asked for prayer, and the power of God came over me. I felt the warmth of God's touch in my body; in fact, it felt as if my whole body was dripping with oil. In that moment, I received a supernatural healing! Since then, I have prayed for and seen many, many people healed in the name of Jesus! I had gained a greater measure of faith and desire to see people receive their own healing.

The year we were 'bleeding', otherwise known as 'our year from hell', was the foundation of an unprecedented year of breakthrough. The following year, we opened a new 1200-seat auditorium. That campus saw over thirty people coming to Christ every week for over a year. The altar was continually filled. Over the next few years, that multi-million-dollar building became debt-free. We saw unprecedented growth in all our church locations, attendance on Sundays was up twenty percent year-on-year every month for the whole year following, and we saw the hand of God blessing our own lives and the lives of our staff. If we refuse to let our pain derail us, it will lead us into greater purpose!

A year of great personal opposition was followed by many years of great blessing: campuses continuing to multiply, another auditorium built in another city virtually debt-free, the purchase of more land to build yet again as well as developing a clear financial roadmap for future buildings, an increasingly capable and Spirit-filled staff and team, the easy flow of innovation, and a new generation of leaders coming through. It was amazing! The foundations of our future were built in our year of pain.

THE LEADER'S TABLE

Side Dishes

CHAPTER TWENTY-ONE

A Table for One, Please

Have you ever been at a restaurant with friends, and over to the side you see someone sitting at a table on their own? It's natural to wonder why they are alone when restaurants are usually a place for celebration, for coming together. It feels out of place to see someone eating at a table for one.

As leaders, we need to be careful that we do not end up isolated and alone. This isn't something we usually do intentionally—it's more of a pattern that creeps in, an indication that something is amiss or not quite right.

Aside from insecurity, there are two main drivers that cause leaders to become isolated: spiritual attack and excessive weariness.

Spiritual Attack

The devil doesn't care how you end up isolated—he just wants to see you eating alone. A spiritual attack is therefore designed to make the leader want to give up. However, if endless trouble comes their way and they still won't quit, Satan will try to diminish the effectiveness of a leader's ministry by isolating them.

There are spiritual and natural reasons we can end up isolated, and both have to be dealt with. As leaders, some time alone is always a good thing, but when we get to a point where we no longer desire to be around people, something is wrong.

Sitting alone at a table for one is the position the enemy of our soul wants us in. He wants us alone with our thoughts; he wants to be the only voice whispering in our ears. Right now, we need to look up and be aware of our surroundings. Are we isolated, or are we in good company?

In our 'year from hell', there was such a strong spiritual attack that John and I found ourselves unexpectedly isolated and alone. For the first time in our twenty years of ministry, we were disconnected from our team. We knew that we were under some form of spiritual attack—we were experiencing health issues, the workload was intense, and many people on our staff and team were discouraged and tired. We had always been a 'hangout church', but suddenly it was as if no one had anything left in the tank. In that season, we found ourselves not wanting to spend time with people. And other people in our lives were pulling back as well. Our morale and that of our team was noticeably dropping. The enemy's strategy was to isolate us, and sure enough, before long we were all doing life alone—which only intensified the spiritual attack.

As the senior leaders, it was up to us to discern what was going on. Realising we were putting a significant stake in the ground and that this was a strategic spiritual attack, we called the church to pray and fast for twenty-one days. Over that time, we experienced incredible breakthrough. Our health was restored, morale returned, but most of all, we became closely connected once again. That year, the church experienced unprecedented growth ... and unity.

Elijah experienced an attack like this. Physically and emotionally, he was depleted. He had experienced great spiritual victories, but suddenly he found himself isolated, vulnerable, and alone. He wasn't just tired and worn out—he was being pursued and threatened by the evil queen Jezebel (1 Kings 19:1-4).

Jezebel's threats had brought so much fear into his life that he ended up running for his life. Elijah was God's man of faith and power for the hour, but now he was petrified. He lost all his courage because of the demonically-inspired utterance of this woman. Right off the back of a season of being powerfully used by God, he came under spiritual attack. This left him isolated, despondent, and even suicidal. After running from the company of others, he ate a solitary meal under a solitary broom tree where he prayed he would die.

Elijah's decision to run from the company of those who could have stood and supported him or held faith for him left him even more vulnerable to the dark thoughts that began to plague his mind. Perhaps the reason depressing thoughts were able to fester in his mind was because there was no counter-narrative in his world when he needed it most. He became even more prone to spiritual attack when he ended up at a table for one.

> He who eats alone, chokes alone.
> – African proverb

Has something made you run away from where God wanted you to be? Has something happened that's making you want to quit? See this for what it is—a spiritual attack. Don't let 'Jezebel' steal your boldness. Don't withdraw to a table for one. Ask some of your trusted leaders to pray for you. Prayer and fasting will break the attack and lift the paralysis from your life. When you most want to isolate, this is the time to force yourself to be with people—not just with anyone, but to intentionally place yourself in the company of Spirit-filled people. The best way to find relief from spiralling thoughts is to run to where there are people who bring perspective, lift you up, and help you regain your fight. The communal table is the answer to spiritual attack.

Right now, if you are isolated and alone, it's time to get up! Leave your table for one. It might feel safe to be alone, but it's not a place of healing and strength. Elijah chose to isolate himself, and as a result, God told him it was time to anoint his successor. This marks a transition point in Elijah's ministry—a handing over of the prophetic mantle—which was possibly sooner than it needed to be.

When we resist the urge to isolate during spiritual attack, the promises God has placed within us are fanned back into life. Rather than being consumed by failure or loss, we need to choose to get among those who are Spirit-filled and can raise us up again.

The woman of Shunem is a great example of this. When her son died, she could have seen it as the death of God's promise to her and fallen into grief. Instead, she got up and travelled in search of the prophet Elisha. She found a man of God who could help in her time of great despair. She did not isolate herself. She sought out people of faith and as a result, a miracle of restoration took place! Because she chose to not remain alone in her moment of greatest vulnerability, her child was raised from the dead! This wasn't only a literal resurrection—for her, it was the resurrection of her dream, a dream she had given birth to and laboured over, a dream she had cared for over many years. It was a dream she could not allow to die.

What is the dream, the purpose, the call God has placed on your life? What promises has He placed in your heart? As a leader, you cannot allow what God has given you to die. Spiritual attacks are real, but we're not meant to deal with them on our own. Seek help to keep going. Seek wise counsel. Seek out those who will contend for you in prayer. We all need support at times. In the face of spiritual attack, retreat is defeat.

Weariness

Another reason leaders begin to isolate themselves is simply because they are feeling weary. When we get tired, it's easy to crave time out. People continually need input and support, and this can take a toll. It's natural to crave an escape from the problems that inevitably come from leading people. But the nature of leadership is that we are only effective when we are inputting into others. Leaders can't lead when they're alone.

Don't avoid the table because you're too busy and tired. Exhaustion can cause us to withdraw from fellowship with others. We can even become so tired we pull back from fellowship with God. We are so busy working *for* God that we begin to resent spending time *with* God. One of the reasons we often get to this point is that our calendars and activities are wearing us out. The weariness is just the result of too much activity. As leaders who love people and love God, we are often the worst at saying no. We also have a tendency to love activity.

At one point in our ministry, John and I realised we had got to a place of deep exhaustion. The ministry hadn't stalled—we just lacked the enthusiasm and energy we'd always had. We'd been trying to keep up with the level of expansion, and we and our team had run hard, but there was very little enthusiasm left. Weariness had set in for some of our key teams and we risked ending up in survival mode. When you only have what it takes to get through the day, the natural thing to do is to preserve what little energy you have left for yourself and your family.

We knew that we couldn't keep doing everything we were doing. Something had to go—and it couldn't be fellowship with one another. We set aside a week, gathered our staff team, and did an audit of all the events we were running. We wrote every activity we were doing as a church on a Post-it note, then placed them in one of three categories: *Stop it, Keep it,* and *Fade it out.* The Post-it notes covered an entire wall.

For three days we deliberated, arguing back and forth over the merit of each activity. Every activity had purpose and was valid. Almost every activity was fruitful. In the end, we made the brutal decision to cut over half our activities. We didn't just cut unproductive activity—we even pulled what was successful. We didn't stop the events because they weren't working; we stopped doing them because we didn't want to further exhaust our team and our leaders. Instead, we found ways to prioritise what was most important and to clarify what God had called us to do as a church. We let go of things that others might have expected us to do and even expectations we'd put on ourselves.

Interestingly, by reducing our level of activity, the yield became far greater. Instead of spreading our resources thin, we pooled our resources and made sure we kept margin in our lives so we could stay true to one of our core values: doing life together.

The takeaway from this is that some of the activities we cling to that are making us tired may be less valuable than we think. Could there be a more time-efficient way of achieving the same outcomes? Could we train someone else to do things in our place, releasing them into the joy of ministry and regaining the time we would have spent doing it ourselves? I guarantee that all of us have things we are doing that we don't really need to do.

At the end of the day, our time and energy for people will be compromised if we are not willing to make hard calls. Instead of being more fruitful, we will become less effective as we are driven into weariness. Jesus came to give us life overflowing, not life running on empty. If we don't deal with the level of activity we create, our lives will spiral out of control. We don't want to be forced to withdraw from people because there is nothing left on the inside of us.

If you are finding yourself isolating from others, take time to reflect on what has got you to this point. Most of us are not wasting our time on ineffective work, but if weariness has set in, make a list of activities you should immediately stop doing, even if they are good and worthwhile.

If there is a spiritual attack in your life, identify who or what has made you feel afraid, vulnerable, or emotionally depleted. Ask God to help you connect with the right people—those who can bring faith to your situation and help break the spiritual attack that is leading to isolation.

You are not meant to do life alone. Avoid retreating to a table for one.

CHAPTER TWENTY-TWO

Complaints About the Menu

Nothing is more demoralising for a leader than dealing with people who have a bad attitude! When everyone seems to be complaining about what's on the menu, it's a sign that ingratitude and negativity have crept in. Unfortunately, whining and complaining are very easy habits to fall into when things aren't going the way we want them to. As leaders, one of our endeavours must be to keep those we lead from becoming complainers.

It is important to note that there is a difference between those who come with a valid complaint and those who have developed an appetite for complaining. While grateful people tend to experience satisfaction, grumblers stir up dissatisfaction. This is why the apostle Paul writes:

Do everything without complaining and arguing.
Philippians 2:14

Gratefulness produces hope and unity, whereas complaining never leads to a good outcome. People who protest, whine and find fault will destroy the future potential of their lives. Great leaders know that an attitude of gratitude is life-changing for them and the community.

In the book of Numbers, God makes it clear that complaining is an attitude that cannot be tolerated in our lives or the lives of others. The Israelites were a nation belonging to God, called to be an example of the greatness of God to the surrounding nations—a display of His glory. They had experienced so much of His goodness and deliverance in their lives. And yet, somewhere along the way on their journey to the promised land, they had turned into a nation of grumblers.

It would be fair to say that the Israelites did have a few things to complain about. They couldn't get new clothes or shoes (I'm sure the fashion-forward set was frustrated wearing the same thing day after day), their meals were repetitive, and they were unsure where God was leading them. They'd left their homes and everything they had ever known. They were in unfamiliar territory. They didn't know what to expect at any given time . . .

But was it really worse to be a free person in the desert than a slave in Egypt?

What started as a few specific complaints, quickly turned rampant. For the Israelites, their complaints became their coffin.

> *Then the Lord said to Moses and Aaron, "How long must I put up with this wicked community and its complaints about me? Yes, I have heard the complaints the Israelites are making against me. Now tell them this: As surely as I live, declares the Lord, I will do to you the very things I heard you say. You will all drop dead in this wilderness! Because you complained against me, every one of you who is twenty years old or older and was included in the registration will die."*
>
> *Numbers 14:26-29*

Rather than rejoicing in their freedom and emancipation, the Israelites complained and romanticised the past. They expressed a complete lack of gratitude for the enormity of what God had done for them in rescuing them from the hand of Pharoah. Convinced that leaving Egypt would be the death of them, their own words dug their shallow graves.

God continually warned them about their grumbling, but they did not listen. And a lot of their complaining was about food! "In Egypt we had all the cucumbers, melons, leeks, onions and garlic we wanted," they said, ". . . but now our appetites are gone. All we ever see is this manna" (Numbers 11:1, 5-7).

Now I understand that these Israelites had only one thing on the menu, but let's be clear: it was manna that fell from heaven! It was *literally* the bread of life!

This is the same manna that was placed in the Ark of the Covenant—and it is the same manna that is promised in the book of Revelation to those who overcome (Revelation 2:17). It is a representation of Jesus Christ. The Israelites were complaining about something very precious that was provided for them by God Himself.

These complainers in the wilderness had lost perspective. Rather than seeing their situation as miraculous and worthy of wonder, they became accusatory, blaming others, resentful of their circumstances, and began acting like victims. They valued their comfort over their calling.

When life gets uncomfortable, we need to keep reminding people of the bigger picture. This is true for us as leaders as well. We need to cling to our calling, even when we have left our comforts behind. We need to be willing to follow the call of God without complaining. Spurgeon wrote:

> "When one's flesh and bones are full of aches and pains, it is as natural for us to murmur as for a horse to shake his head when the flies tease him . . . but nature should not be the rule with Christians, or what is their religion worth?"

The Israelites had become 'doorway dwellers'. Instead of making progress towards the promised land or being productive along the way, they stood around in the doorways of their tents, complaining. They let their attitude inhibit their aptitude for action. They weren't preparing for what lay ahead or focussing on God's goodness and faithful provision. They didn't have a bias towards action. They had lists of complaints with no solutions. They entertained wishful thinking over being resourceful. They were meant to be a people full of purpose. Instead, they had become a bunch of navel-gazing divas.

Not only was God very angry with their complaining, but Moses was aggravated too! In Numbers 11 we read:

> *Moses heard all the families standing in the doorways of their tents whining, and the Lord became extremely angry. Moses was also very aggravated. And Moses said to the Lord, "Why are you treating me, your servant, so harshly? Have mercy on me! What did I do to deserve the burden of all these people? Did I give birth to them? Did I bring them into the world? Why did you tell me to carry them in my arms like a mother carries a nursing baby? How can I carry them to the land you swore to give their ancestors? Where am I supposed to get meat for all these people? They keep whining to me, saying, 'Give us meat to eat!' I can't carry all these people by myself! The load is far too heavy! If this is how you intend to treat me, just go ahead and kill me. Do me a favor and spare me this misery!"*
>
> *Numbers 11:10-15*

This is a powerful example of leadership. While the people are complaining to Moses about anything and everything, Moses is bringing his complaint to the Lord. How is he meant to lead all these whiners and moaners?

This is the amazing thing—God does not dismiss the issue or minimise Moses' complaint. Instead, He gives Moses an action plan. "Appoint more people as elders to carry the load" (v. 16-17). God acknowledges that Moses has a valid complaint and provides him with a solution. God will always hear and respond to our complaints.

This is where we need to teach people to take their complaints—to God. David said, "I pour out all my complaints before him and tell him all my troubles" (Psalm 142:2). The Israelites took their complaints to each other, but what did it achieve? It created dissatisfaction and unrest for the people and their leaders. In contrast, Moses and David and all the great leaders of the Bible knew the power and the wisdom of taking their complaints to the Lord. They had learned to trust God. When a person keeps on complaining, even if the complaint seems valid, it reflects a lack of trust in God. Such people soon lose their joy in leadership.

If only the Israelites had seen that if they just kept moving forward, God would have their back! He had stopped the Egyptian army from chasing them, He was their front and rear guard. The only danger in their lives was their stinking thinking. The most telling thing about their attitude is that they had quit on God.

Complainers are quitters. The Israelites quit on God's plan to conquer the promised land when it was so close they could see it. All the complainers did indeed die in the wilderness. Grumbling and complaining took out an entire generation.

How awful for people to get so close to fulfilling God's purpose and then not make it because their attitude took them out! As leaders, we need to allow people to bring a complaint if there is a genuine problem. Together we can create an action plan to solve the problem. We also need to empower people to take their complaints to the Lord, to lift their eyes to the call and promise on their lives, and to help them cultivate a heart of gratitude.

Sometimes our complaints come because we are not being treated the way we think we deserve. Gratitude and thankfulness are attitudes borne from humility. A grateful person is a humble person as they recognise that God has treated them better than they ever deserved. The best way to rid ourselves of a complaining attitude is to be actively thankful. It's the people who, even in the worst circumstances, find something to be grateful for, that leave a mark in history.

CHAPTER TWENTY-THREE

Squabbles at Supper

How do you establish a team that plays nicely with each other? How do you get people to celebrate each other's gifts and talents and not become competitive or threatened by each other? The leadership dream is to have a team who become best friends, a team of people who don't see themselves as competitors but as companions.

Some people, perhaps subconsciously, have adopted a way of leading characterised by 'divide and rule', where they play people off against each other. Leaders like this tend to mock or pull down team members behind their backs and publicly highlight their failings. This creates division, with everyone competing for the leader's approval. The greatest challenge these team members face is the feeling that they are in competition with or comparing themselves with each other, when God has placed them alongside each other to benefit one another.

A team that works together well is one where a leader celebrates the contributions and wins of every member of the team. It is usually when people feel unloved, unappreciated or overlooked that we see infighting take place and division amongst the team.

Leaders identify and celebrate every person's unique contribution. The team dynamic we must establish as leaders is that there is no competition among us. We win and lose together. Sometimes people end up competing and comparing over something that is not even their calling! They know this is futile, but this often occurs when their place and role on the team are not clear. As leaders, part of what we do is help people see the importance of their gifts and talents and help each other identify and value their contribution to the team.

Leaders create camaraderie. In the kingdom of God, it is a key principle that we are stronger together. The world presents a picture of winning and success that is often about an individual rising to the top. In the kingdom, however, we are to look not only to our own interests but also to the interests of others (Philippians 2:4). God's purpose for each person is amplified as they live it out in relationship with others. We are not to play off one person against the other but to help everyone walk in their calling with confidence and strength, encouraging each other in their gifts and releasing the people in our teams to flourish.

We must recognise that allowing a competitive spirit among our teams is a trap. We need to learn to build relationally strong teams. It's very sad when we see infighting and broken relationships because it doesn't have to be the case.

Rachel and Leah are two sisters in the Bible who could have made an amazing team. Both were part of God's unfolding plan and could have been incredible companions. Instead, they spent their lives as competitors. They were constantly 'squabbling at supper'.

Rachel and Leah definitely didn't have it easy. They were not happy about being married to the same man (talk about a recipe for disaster), but they had little choice in the matter. Right from the start of their marriage, Leah experienced incredibly painful rejection. She knows she is the unwanted and unloved sister. Despite this lack of favour, Leah gets pregnant and starts having children while Rachel remains barren. Rachel is torn up with jealousy (Genesis 30:1). Her competitiveness to have children—and their joint vying for Jacob's attention and affection—causes the two sisters to work against each other rather than work together. Even though their situation was difficult, they could have chosen to handle it with grace toward each other.

If there are a lot of squabbles in our leadership environments, is it because we are not being fair? Are we displaying favouritism toward one person over another? Is it that we are praising one person and overlooking the other? Favouritism is not always something we are fully aware of. Rachel and Leah could have had a harmonious relationship as peers and equals, but because Jacob displayed favouritism toward Rachel they became competitive, manipulative, and badly behaved. You can almost hear the triumph in Rachel's voice when her servant Bilhah finally conceives a child, which makes the baby Rachel's:

> *I have had a great struggle with my sister,* **and I have won.**
> *Genesis 30:8 NIV*

The reality is, however, Rachel hadn't won—she had lost. She had lost the one who could have been her greatest friend, her best companion, an ally with her at all times. She was viewing life from the wrong perspective.

If only Rachel and Leah could have found a way to get on together. They were sisters, they were peers, they were in each other's world constantly, but they were unwilling to trust each other or open up to each other.

Are there people we see as threats or competitors when we could embrace them as our family? A healthy team is similar to a well-functioning family. Team relationships must fundamentally start with trust. The companionship and bonding of a team are found in being transparent with one another. The teams we lead should be a safe place for people to bare their souls, to reveal who they truly are. When people are vulnerable with one another, squabbling and competition lose their attraction. It's hard to stab someone in the back if you're looking them in the face! A great leader ensures those they lead do not use each other's weaknesses against each other but love and support each other despite their weaknesses.

Jesus embodied this kind of leadership. He would not allow His followers to whitewash their lives or be hypocrites. With Jesus among them, the disciples did not need to pretend. They could be fully transparent with each other, walking through life with honesty and humility.

Leaders create synergy. It's not reasonable or realistic to expect that there will be no disagreements or differing viewpoints when we lead a team of people. If members of a team never disagree, there's probably a level of false harmony, which is even more of a concern. As leaders, it's our job to draw out what is in people whether that's in keeping with the party line or not. We're not threatened by those who disagree—in fact, we welcome honest and open conversations. Our desire is for teams to work through their differences together and be willing to resolve issues and come to a point of agreement.

Squabbles are more easily settled when the relationships within the team are seen as important as the outcomes. This happens when teams don't just work together, they also play together.

Creating a truly bonded team takes time. We can't microwave our team relationships. We have to foster them and build environments for the friendships to deepen. As leaders, we are not threatened when the team forms close bonds with each other—we are deeply encouraged because that's how it's meant to be! This is where we need to get intentional.

Here are some characteristics of teams that grow together and become more effective over time:

1. ***They have meals together.*** (Hopefully by now you predicted that!)
   They enjoy food and fellowship. As the saying goes, "After a good dinner, one can forgive anybody, even one's own relatives."

2. ***They have fun together.*** As leaders, we need to assign part of our budget to team activities that are simply fun, knowing that shared experiences help people form deep bonds. Usually, some memorable moments will be created that live beyond that day.
3. ***They share cares and tears.*** By leading with vulnerability and openness about the challenges and struggles, we create a safe place for the team to be able to open their heart to each other.
4. ***They pray and prophesy over each other.*** There's nothing like people praying for one another to unite hearts. Hearing from God for one another deepens our love for each other. Some of our most powerful moments leading teams have been when the Holy Spirit has moved and things have shifted.

There are also some key characteristics of leaders who nurture healthy teams:

1. ***They have the good of the whole team at heart.*** A leader regularly checks—is there anything that could cause division, such as favouritism or overlooking contributions?
2. ***They celebrate each person.*** Leaders are specific and deliberate about honouring the team players and highlighting their importance in the team.
3. ***They overlook offences.*** Leaders love their team with everything they have. When we model love for those we lead, that love will be replicated in the team.

There is nothing quite like being on a team where competitiveness gives way to companionship and squabbles give way to synergy. When this happens and everyone begins to play their part, others want to join in and the team soon takes on unprecedented momentum.

THE LEADER'S TABLE

Specials:

CHAPTER TWENTY-FOUR

Five Thousand for Dinner? No Problem!

Do you ever get sick and tired of the constant issues that arise in leadership? Perhaps you know the feeling—the great things you are doing for God are increasing, but the problems are rapidly on the increase too.

One fine day, Jesus was preaching to crowds of people who had flocked to hear Him. They'd been listening for hours on end, but the day was coming to a close. The problem was, they were in a remote area. With no McDonalds or Chick-fil-A nearby, what would they do for food? Five thousand men, as well as women and children, needed to eat. That's a lot of hungry people.

The disciples saw the problem. Turning to Jesus, they said:

> *This is a remote place, and it's already getting late. Send the crowds away so they can go to the villages and buy food for themselves.*
> Matthew 14:15

But Jesus replied, "That isn't necessary—you feed them" (v. 16). In other words, "You can solve this problem. You have the ability to overcome this challenge."

This led to questioning among the disciples. Where would they get food to feed this many people? The disciples had walked with Jesus long enough that they should have been thinking outside the box by now. Their faith should have grown to the point where they expected God to come through. Instead, they were limited by what they could see in front of them. They were still thinking quite naturally.

The disciples couldn't come up with a solution, but Jesus could. Taking one small picnic offering, He multiplies it and feeds a multitude. Food came out of thin air, materialising in such abundant quantities that no one went home hungry that day. Leaders are those who see a problem—and find a way to solve it.

Sometimes in leadership, it seems like the problems never let up. No sooner have we dealt with one issue, than another arises. It can get totally overwhelming. *How can we get rid of these issues? How can we solve all the problems that are continually presenting themselves?*

It changes everything when we realise that rather than constantly pushing us down, problems are a pathway into greater spiritual territory. Problems are the leader's passport, taking them into new levels of victory. The height to which you go in leadership will be determined by the level of problem you can solve.

The key is that as the problems get more complex, our faith needs to grow in proportion. The bigger the problem, the greater the faith we need.

Jacob the Overcomer

Think about Jacob for a moment (Genesis 32). Jacob struggled his whole life. You think you have problems—Jacob's issues started in the womb! Before he takes his first breath, his twin brother is fighting him. It's quite a conversation-piece, how much Rebecca is suffering as they tussle in her belly. It wasn't normal 'twin behaviour'. The womb is meant to be a peaceful environment, but that wasn't the case for Jacob.

His next problem came while he was being born. With his brother, Esau, beating him out of the birth canal, thereby gaining the rights of the firstborn son, Jacob begins his life with a chip on his shoulder.

From there, he has problem after problem. He struggles in his relationship with his dad, his boss (who is also his father-in-law . . . it's complicated), and then he experiences two women fighting over him, treating him like he's a piece of meat. Jacob spent his life wrestling and struggling.

And then Jacob encounters a problem he can't wrestle his way through. He's dealt with everything he can so far, but now Esau is on his way to meet him, and Jacob is afraid for his life.

Is this to be his lot in life, encountering problem after problem, or does something have to break in him for this pattern to change? Surrounded by trouble, Jacob removes himself and goes to a place where he is alone. There, God comes to wrestle it out with Jacob. This is a defining moment in his life. From this night on, Jacob's struggles will no longer limit him. They will unlock his future.

That night, Jacob comes face to face with his challenges, his vulnerability, and his fears. During his struggle to surrender to God, God asks Jacob a surprising question. "What is your name?" The last time he was asked that question, Jacob lied to his father saying, "I am Esau." All his life, Jacob has been trying to get ahead by his own wiles and strategies. He is used to finding solutions of his own making. But not anymore. If Jacob is to become the patriarch of faith he is destined to be, something in him has to break.

God is asking Jacob, "Will you admit who you are and let me change you? Will you admit you can't do it on your own?" In that moment, Jacob surrenders to God and his name is changed to Israel.

> *"Your name will no longer be Jacob," the man told him.*
> *"From now on you will be called Israel, because you*
> *have fought with God and with men and have won."*
> Genesis 32:28

Jacob has been overwhelmed and overcome his whole life, but in one encounter with God, he becomes an overcomer. His original name meant 'grasps at man's heel'. Now his name is Israel, which means 'triumphant with God' or 'prevails with God'.

During that night of struggle, Jacob finally realises he needs to stop resisting God and surrender all his problems to Him. He discovers the greatest struggle is not to do things without God, but to hold tightly to God and seek his blessing. That night, Jacob goes from success based on his own schemes and wiliness, to success based on his grasp of God, and God's favour on his life. As Israel, he was now a massive part of God's plan and purposes on the earth.

In the wrestle with God, Jacob's hip was crippled. Jacob experienced what G. Campbell Morgan called "the crippling that crowns." When God has our surrender, He can trust us with his power. To be an overcomer, we first need to allow God to overcome us. Success starts in surrender, not in fighting. As we surrender to the Lordship of Christ, we may find that the problems that threaten to cripple us are used by God to crown us.

Leaders are Overcomers

When I was about eighteen years old, I saw a vision in prayer that I have carried with me ever since. In my vision, I saw a thick bush, incredibly dense, that had no pathway through it. As I watched, I saw myself cutting a path with a bright, gleaming silver sword. It was not easy going. I was getting exhausted and I was dirty and sweaty, but I was persisting. As I was cutting the path and wondering, *why am I doing this?*, I was prompted to look behind me. Suddenly, I saw why it mattered. Behind me was a large company of people, a surprising number, freely walking on the path that I had just cut.

I received this vision at a time when I was facing an obstacle I couldn't get through, but it has stayed with me ever since. To this day, I am committed to dealing with the terrain in front of me and clearing a path for others. Why? Because I have seen who follows behind. That vision has inspired me to keep going even when I have wanted to give up.

Overcomers are those who do not give up. Overcomers never quit. As leaders, we will face obstacles and we may need to cut a new path, but with the power and anointing of God, we can make a way through any challenge. Whenever we overcome, we create a pathway for others to follow in our footsteps. As leaders, we need to recognise that:

- every problem can be overcome
- wrestling is part of our leadership development
- some problems need to be surrendered to Christ Jesus
- we have the spirit of Christ, which is the spirit of an overcomer

One quality of a great leader is that they have an overcoming spirit that comes from faith. We become bigger than our problems when we understand that no situation can defeat our faith. Jesus expected His disciples to be able to give the crowd food. He wanted them to get to the point where they overcame problems because they shared the same spirit as Him.

> *Everyone born of God overcomes the world. This is the victory that has overcome the world, even our faith.*
> 1 John 5:4 NIV

We serve an overcoming God, and He wants us to overcome! Overcoming faith starts in our mind with what we believe is possible. We have to think right, to fight our problems right. We are overcomers! In Christ, we can overcome obstacles, tests, failures, unbelief, fear, challenges, and any other issue we face. Everything is solvable! God can solve every challenge. Leadership is about accepting that we will constantly have something to overcome, some problem that needs to be solved. We need to realise we are still winning even if there are things yet to be resolved. We need to allow God to enlarge our spirit to become who we need to be. There is no problem that is greater than God, so we must increase our faith to believe that there is a way through.

Some issues are resolved with time. Others need to be faced head-on. But most of the problems we face in leadership are an opportunity to grow our faith, expand our capacity, and take new ground. Our leadership will grow to the level we are willing to deal with the problems other people can't. Overcoming faith makes what was impossible, possible. Did you know that Jesus laid a table for thousands of hungry people more than once? He fed 5,000 and he fed 4,000. He solved this problem again and again. When you do it once you can do it again!

Let's have an overcoming spirit that comes from faith. Let's be those who say, "I am bigger than my problems" because "greater is He who is in me than he who is in the world" (1 John 4:4). Believe that you will see the victory. God has it all in hand! Jesus said, "In this world you will have trouble. But take heart! I have overcome the world" (John 16:33).

CHAPTER TWENTY-FIVE

Food in Famine

One of the hallmarks of a great leader is their faith. To build anything requires faith, to keep building requires faith, to endure hard times requires faith, to give God the glory in success requires faith.

When John and I knew God was calling us to start a church, a phrase from the movie, *Field of Dreams* began resonating in our spirits. In the movie, the lead character, a huge baseball fan, gets a vision to build a baseball field in his backyard. It's an outrageous concept. And then he hears a voice: "If you build it, they will come." The moment John and I heard that line, we felt the Holy Spirit was saying the same thing to us. Full of faith, we did just that—we went ahead and built a church!

Faith is the substance God uses to build something from nothing. We were completely unknown in the city God called us to, we had no stake in the ground, but we placed our faith in God, and over time, He truly did build something out of nothing. We didn't need anything more than a word from God.

God will always resource leaders who act in faith. We are not at the mercy of circumstances. We don't live bound to the economies and possibilities of this world. We lean into the provision of God! A faith-filled leader functions under a supernatural, open heaven where all things are possible, and they believe that God can work in mysterious ways. God wants to provide resources and blessing for His people! He wants us to have all that we need to outwork His purpose.

> *And God is able to bless you abundantly, so that*
> *in all things at all times, having all that you*
> *need, you will abound in every good work.*
> 2 Corinthians 9:8 NIV

How do we see this abundance in our lives? By partnering with God in our faith. As leaders, we must never allow natural circumstances to dictate what we believe is supernaturally possible. In the Bible, we see God miraculously providing food for His people time and time again. Food in famine, manna in the wilderness . . . even birds can be used to bring an Uber-eats delivery of food to a prophet!

Joseph's Faith

Joseph was in some of the worst circumstances imaginable, yet he found faith to lead wherever he was placed. Everything in his sphere of authority always flourished.

Joseph had the dream of leadership in his heart from his earliest years; he had God's word on his life. Yet nothing in the natural aligned with that dream. As a teenager, Joseph was sold into slavery by his jealous brothers. In Egypt, he brought blessing to Potiphar's house only to be sent to prison having been unfairly accused. But even as a prisoner, Joseph was elevated by God. He gained respect and influence . . . and leadership opportunities!

What is the key that caused Joseph to prosper? Despite his terrible circumstances, he never wavered in his faith in God. His faith held him steady, positioned him, and set him up for what should have been impossible leadership influence.

Joseph's faith in God's promises for him meant that when famine struck, Joseph was already positioned and resourced to provide for God's chosen people. Thanks to his faith and his willingness to trust God in difficult times, the Israelites had access to an abundance of food during a crippling famine.

Faith-filled leaders enable others not just to survive, but to thrive! They hear a word from God, hold onto it in faith, and apply wisdom in every situation. Acting on what he heard, Joseph brought all of his experience, his leadership intuition, and a God-breathed strategy so that not just he and his people, but the nations around, had an abundance of food in a time of famine.

> Don't settle for crumbs when God has laid a table.

Joseph's faith grew to the point where it wasn't just his life that was saved and blessed. The people of Egypt recognised that they would have died without Joseph's leadership. They saw that God was with him and knew that without him the famine would have ended their lives. He was appointed to leadership by God "for the saving of many lives" (Genesis 50:20 NIV).

Joseph's largeness of faith meant that God's people were not just fed, but set up to multiply and prosper. Bringing his entire family from Canaan, he settled them in Egypt. God placed this small family of seventy people into the womb of Egypt for four hundred years—the perfect place where He could build them into a nation. Joseph's faith created a way for the nation of Israel to be resourced for generations to come.

Elijah's Faith

Later in the Old Testament, we read about another famine. For three and a half years, the heavens were closed. The lack of rain had created a lack of food.

Naturally, people had reached a point of desperation. They had no more faith to cling to. One woman in particular had come to the end of herself.

But God brings a man of faith onto the scene. And again, faith unlocks heaven's resources. Elijah is sent to the widow with a strategy that will save her life and resource her family for years to come. Following his instructions, she sets about to make him some bread. "Don't be afraid," he said, "Do what I've said." Then he gives her a promise from God:

> *There will always be flour and olive oil left in*
> *your containers until the time when the Lord*
> *sends rain and the crops grow again!*
> 1 Kings 17:14

Elijah heard and acted on a word from God, and as a result, provision flowed. A closed heaven became an open heaven, a place of God's blessing and miracles.

Like Elijah, leaders should have food in famine because they have learned how to live under an open heaven. Even before God sent Elijah to the widow, he ensured that Elijah was being supplied with food (in the most unusual manner!).

> *Drink from the brook and eat what the ravens bring*
> *you, for I have commanded them to bring you food.*
> 1 Kings 17:4

A leader who follows God will find that their needs are always met. God does not abandon us when we are outworking His will. Quite the opposite—our needs are met, not just in our circumstances, but *in spite of* our circumstances. How amazing that God used scavenger birds to bring food to Elijah! Ravens never part with their food! But that's the dynamic of an open heaven. Things that aren't even on the table in the natural begin to overflow supernaturally.

Many leaders become discouraged when they feel heaven is closed over their lives and ministries. They long for the presence of God, for a touch of the Holy Spirit. They desire to see the hand of God moving in their lives. Instead, it feels like they are living under a cloud. They become full of doubt, they often experience lack and frustration. This is not what God has in mind. God's will is that every leader has plenty—not just for themselves, but enough to give away, to be a blessing. God never sets a bare table. Even in the presence of our enemies, He creates a lavish feast.

Joseph and Elijah both lived at a time when the heavens were closed. What set them apart as leaders was that they sought the Lord and responded to His voice. They didn't fight against the circumstances they were in but surrendered to God's will in every place. They went where God told them to go even when it didn't make sense. And by doing this—in pits and prisons and alongside little brooks—they grew their faith and unlocked God's provision.

When we live under an open heaven, nothing can stand in the way of God's supply and favour falling on our lives. Under an open heaven we live in abundance, and what we do has an overflowing impact.

If as leaders we are to provide food in famine, we must live from a place of revelation. We are not to lean on human reasoning or come up with our own strategy. There is a supernatural clarity that cuts through the confusion. We see the potential and possibilities we have in God. We store up food, creating a rich supply in our storehouse ready to give away. If we have faith in God, nothing can erode our supply.

What is the vision God has given you? What has He asked you to build?
He will provide strength when you feel weary.
He will provide encouragement when you feel low.
He will provide certainty in uncertain times.
He will provide the people to help you outwork His purpose.
He will provide the resources.

He will provide all that is needed for the vision to flourish.

He will provide whatever you lack.

Have faith that God will provide for every need.

As leaders, we know what it is to have food in times of famine.

CHAPTER TWENTY-SIX

Dinner with the Devil

"But here at this table, sitting among us as a friend, is the man who will betray me."
Luke 22:21

Jesus' last act before He was betrayed was to dine with His closest friends and disciples. Among them that night sat the one who would betray Him. We read, "... when Judas had eaten the bread, Satan entered into him" (John 13:27).

Jesus had the devil at the dinner table.

One of the things that can easily take us out in our leadership journey is when we experience the pain of betrayal. Jesus knew that He was the sacrificial lamb, that He had come to die in our place. He knew that Judas would be His betrayer from the beginning—He knew Judas would push Him towards the cross.

This is made clear in John's gospel:

Jesus ... knew all people. He did not need any testimony about mankind, for he knew what was in each person.
John 2:24-25

"Did I not choose you, the twelve? And yet one of you is a devil". He spoke of Judas the son of Simon Iscariot, for he, one of the twelve, was going to betray him.
John 6:70-71 ESV

∼

Judas was part of Jesus' inner circle. He had been close enough, for long enough, that he was on the invite list for the Last Supper. He made it into that sacred room.

Jesus' ultimate betrayal did not come at the hands of a stranger—it came at the hands of one He had done life with, broken bread with, travelled and ministered on the road with. Judas had seen everything that Jesus had done; he had seen His integrity and righteousness first-hand. If even the perfect nature and character of Jesus were not enough to hold back his betrayal, why would we think that we, with all our faults and failings, will not also experience betrayal at some point in our ministry?

It's a sad reality that the people we love the most hold the power to hurt us the most. The closer someone is to us, the more it hurts when they let us down or turn on us. The irony of Judas' betrayal is that he did it with a kiss. The act of betrayal he used was an act of greeting and warmth. Not all betrayals look the way they feel. There are actions that on the surface seem innocuous—comments people make that don't sound too bad but if we were to dig beneath the surface, the subtext is not good—things that appear to be casually said and done but cut deeper into a leader than others might perceive...

Firstly, we must settle in our hearts that as leaders we will never knowingly play the part of Judas ourselves. We never want to betray those closest to us. To avoid this, we must choose not to gossip about what people are going through. We don't share people's confidences with those who don't need to know. We make it a non-negotiable that we will 'tame' our tongue. Avoiding gossip will keep us from betraying those we serve alongside.

In leadership circles, I'm amazed at how gossip invariably gets back to the person who was spoken about. It never stays 'just between us'. Most of the people who want 'the goss' are likely to enjoy the power found in spreading 'the goss'. Let's not betray one another by having loose lips. Gossip is horrible. God hates it, it causes division, and it ruins relationships.

Secondly, we must watch that we don't let a spirit of judgment cloud our view of those we lead with. Often a betrayal is preceded by a judgment. When we judge a person in light of what we know and according to our own measuring stick, we're less likely to feel bad about betraying them. It's easy to alleviate any feelings of guilt when we set ourselves up as judge and jury. Jesus warns us not to judge others. The truth is, we could be in a weaker place than they are but we just can't see it.

This is so important for a leader. We must not sit in the seat of judgement. We don't take the place of the accuser. We don't betray our friends.

But what do we do when we are the one who is betrayed?

It's a difficult thing for a leader to realise they have been betrayed. Betrayal is always personal, but when it comes from those we've loved and trusted, even from those we have invited to sit alongside us at the leadership table, it hurts on a whole other level.

We must learn the difference between hurt and pain.

The hurt is what has been done to us. The pain is what we experience. Both have the potential to sideline us and turn us from our ultimate destiny.

The only way to deal with hurt is to let go of it. We can't afford to keep reliving the words that were said. We can't keep replaying the script that took place. We can't allow ourselves to memorise the moments. If we do, the hurt will harden in our hearts. This is how hurt solidifies into offence. As leaders, we are to respond in love, and love overlooks every offence. To overlook is to be willing to not focus or dwell on what has happened. We are to look past what has been said and done.

This is not easy. I wish it was. But like everything we do as Christians, this is a choice we must make for our own emotional, mental and spiritual health. Hurt simply has to be let go of or it will end up destroying us. When we choose not to dwell on how we were hurt and instead turn our attention to life-giving topics, our conversations become so much more exciting. Rather than looking backwards and focusing on the past, we can move forward.

Pain is different. Pain is something we embrace, knowing it can produce beauty in us. Beauty can come from ashes, and the Bible teaches us we can rejoice in the middle of suffering. There is a test of our leadership in a time of betrayal: *Will we allow hurt to make us bitter, or will we allow pain to make us better?*

Pain can make us more like Christ. When we experience pain, we come to know more of Him and understand the leadership pain He felt as the son of suffering. In our suffering, we can become like Him. In Christ, the pain we experience can turn into joy.

Jesus . . . for the joy that was set before him endured the cross.
Hebrews 12:2

When we experience betrayal, we must choose to fully forgive. Jesus forgave Judas. He forgave every one of us who through our sinful nature nailed Him to the cross. His mercy and forgiveness are now our example and our expectation—we must forgive as we have been forgiven.

Betrayal is the ultimate test of our character. Will we choose to forgive? Will we stop picking at the scab? Will we stop looking for a way to discuss our injury with anyone willing to listen? Will we choose to understand why that person behaved the way they did? Will we accept any responsibility we had for why they did what they did?

The one thing we must never do is seek revenge. Now, I must admit that I do enjoy a good revenge movie. Revenge movies are so gratifying to watch!

Sometimes the characters get so carried away with exacting justice that they lose all self-control and just become cold-hearted killing machines.

Revenge, or vengeance, is never ours—it belongs to God. We will limit the level of our leadership and put a ceiling over our lives if we become intent on revenge. I'm sure none of us would resort to physical violence, but it's so easy to seek revenge in other ways. Don't become a keyboard warrior. Don't let your words reveal the lack of forgiveness in your heart. Trust that God will be at work in your betrayer's life and entrust your reputation to Him.

It's not lost on me that Judas' final betrayal of Jesus was carried out in an olive grove. Olive oil is only released through crushing. There is an increased anointing on us when we have experienced crushing in leadership.

You prepare a table before me in the presence of my enemies.
You anoint my head with oil, my cup overflows.
Psalm 23:5 NIV

Let go of the betrayal. Let go of the hurt. Forgive them. Own your part. Move forward.

Jesus was willing to do this—even with the one who broke bread with Him, then broke His heart.

CHAPTER TWENTY-SEVEN

Turning Stones Into Bread

As our lives and ministries go to new levels, we will find that specific leadership temptations come our way. How we deal with these temptations is vital to maintaining our authority and trustworthiness before God and man.

It seems unthinkable, but Jesus was tempted in three specific ways:

> *Then Jesus was led by the Spirit into the wilderness to be tempted by the devil. After fasting forty days and forty nights, he was hungry. The tempter came to him and said,* **"If you are the Son of God, tell these stones to become bread."** *Then the devil took him to the holy city and had him stand on the highest point of the temple.* **"If you are the Son of God,"** *he said,* **"throw yourself down . . ."** *Again, the devil took him to a very high mountain and showed him all the kingdoms of the world and their splendour.* **"All this I will give you,"** *he said,* **"if you will bow down and worship me."**
> *Matthew 4:1-11 NIV*

If Jesus was tempted and His leadership and calling were on the line, then the same thing can happen to us. When we are aware of the specific leadership temptations Satan offered to Jesus, we can be wary of them. The devil tried to derail and tempt Jesus in three key ways:

The 'Stones To Bread' Temptation

In Matthew 4:2 we read that Jesus has been fasting for forty days and forty nights, and He is hungry—no doubt a serious understatement. This fast has been very significant for Jesus. It marked His dedication and devotion to the call on His life and was an important part of being set apart for His ministry. When the devil comes, he tries to appeal to Jesus' flesh. He wants the flesh—the physical body's needs and demands—to be preeminent. If Jesus' physical self-control can fail, then the devil will be able to use this temptation again.

Jesus refuses to allow the flesh to hold sway. He doesn't give in to His physical desires or needs. Instead, the spirit overcomes the flesh. This is important for us as leaders. We cannot overcome our flesh through our flesh. We must choose *by the Spirit* to overcome the desires of our flesh.

The other aspect of this temptation is whether Jesus would use His anointing to benefit Himself. The devil is essentially saying to Jesus, "You have the anointing, don't you? Feed yourself!" He wants Jesus to use His power, His anointing, for personal gain. Jesus knew He had the power to create food, He knew that He had transformational power, but He knew it was not for Himself that the power was given. He could not abuse the gift of God for personal gain.

As leaders, situations will arise where it is possible to use what God has given us to benefit ourselves and to get what we want. In these moments we are to resist the devil. We are not here to feed ourselves but to feed others.

I have been incredibly blessed throughout my life to lead many generous and selfless people—people who volunteer their skills, time and energy, serving and giving to see God move. I have done all I can to never abuse that generosity or to personally gain from it. I aim to be the giver in my relationships more than being a taker.

It has been incredibly humbling when people have volunteered their time and energy to help me personally. But this has never come from deploying a 'ministry of hints'. As leaders, we have to work hard to avoid using people. John and I have always been incredibly aware that we are 'co-workers' and 'co-heirs' of Christ with every person we lead. We play our part to the best of our ability, as do they. It's easy for people to conflate serving a leader with serving God. In light of this, we must be careful not to use people or to place unrealistic expectations on them. We must recognise the temptation to take advantage of our leadership position and ensure that what we ask of people has kingdom significance.

The 'Throw Yourself Down' Temptation

In the second temptation given to Jesus, the devil tells Him if He is the Son of God, He should throw Himself down from a cliff. The devil wants Jesus to question His identity. In this and the previous temptation he begins with the same words: "If you are . . ."

His goal is to make Jesus doubt Himself, to feel like He has to prove who He is. The devil is trying to appeal to a sense of self-importance. He wants to undermine Jesus' confidence. But Jesus simply knew who He was—and He had no need to prove it.

The devil wants us to question who we are in God, to question our calling. As leaders, we don't need to prove who we are, we don't need to elevate ourselves or praise ourselves. We need to let God's hand on our lives be our only endorsement. Our temptation is not to 'throw ourselves off a cliff' but that at times we would verbally 'throw ourselves down' in front of people, looking for them to affirm us or lift us with their words. When we begin looking for people to speak into who we are or to give us praise and encouragement to build us up and make us feel significant or special, we need to be careful. We must recognise the temptation to become leaders who feed on the praise of the people rather than the approval and pleasure of God.

Some people get on a stage and suddenly become 'crowd drunk'. They feed off being the centre of attention and become caught up in themselves. These people tend to be the hero of every story they tell; every success can be ascribed to their contribution. These are the ones that run out the clock on their allotted time, taking liberties to decide how much time they deserve. I may have taken on a less-than-glowing tone as I describe this, but it is unpleasant when we witness this.

The devil is tempting Jesus to act with an inflated sense of importance. What's ironic about this temptation is that Jesus *is* the centre! He *is* so important! Jesus is the Lamb of God who takes away the sin of the world (John 1:29 NIV). He is the one found worthy to open the scroll (Revelation 5:9). He *is* the centre—he doesn't have to *try* to be the centre! Jesus is the centre of time, the centre of human history, the centre of the universe.

> "... in him all things hold together."
> *Colossians 1:17 NIV*

Yet it is precisely because He didn't grasp hold of the central place that Jesus became central. While He was here on earth, He understood that He wasn't here to be protected, He wasn't here to be looked after—He was here to be the servant of all. For a leader, it's about knowing that our importance is in the calling God gives us, not in the recognition we receive.

The 'All This I Will Give You' Temptation

In the third temptation, the devil takes Jesus to a high mountain where he shows Him the kingdoms of the world and their splendour. He offers to give them all to Jesus if He will simply bow down and worship him. This is crazy!

The devil is trying to offer Jesus what He is already going to achieve by dying on the cross. The devil is seemingly offering Jesus a far easier path to achieve His goal. He's saying, "Get what you want without the sacrifice. Build a legacy by taking a shortcut!"

But Jesus knew that leadership is not given, it's earned. The lasting legacy we build is based on what we surrender and sacrifice. Jesus said, "I lay down my life for the sheep" (John 10:15). He knew there was no shortcut to fulfilling His purpose. Jesus knew that all the kingdoms of the world would one day be handed to Him. Why? Because of His great sacrifice! He was not prepared to sacrifice His calling on the altar of comfort.

This temptation was also a test of ownership. Jesus wasn't on earth to build His own kingdom—He was here to build His Father's kingdom. Jesus wasn't motivated by what He would get—He was here for His Father's glory.

The devil will always try to sell us ownership of a much smaller allotment in God than we can actually have. We are *heirs* of the kingdom, we *inherit* the kingdom! It is no small inheritance that Jesus died to give us. Jesus was aware that what the devil offered was only a small measure of God's creation. He knew that one day all things would be put under His feet (Ephesians 1:22).

Whose kingdom are you building? This is a question every leader has to come to terms with. We are not here to build our own little kingdom—we are here to build God's kingdom. We only have what we have already been entrusted with. As leaders, our ministry, our churches, our teams are not ours—they are given to us to steward and then give back again. We must see that even the people we raise up are never ours—they are always His. We are never to think of them as 'our leaders'.

We live blessed lives when we know that nothing we have is truly ours and that everything we have belongs to Him. The house we live in, the children we raise, the church we build, the ministry we are part of, the wealth we have, the work we lead ... if we think it is ours, we think far too small. Jesus didn't want things for Himself; He wanted to serve God's purposes.

We are not here to claim ownership of the things of this world but to lay up a reward in heaven that is of eternal value. We know we are only winning if the kingdom is winning.

～

If we can pass these three leadership temptations—not using the anointing for our benefit; being secure, not self-important; and, building God's kingdom not our own—I believe we will step into a new level of authority and impact. It was directly after He passed these tests that Jesus' public ministry began. Soon after the temptation, He called the disciples and began to build the foundations of the early church. Jesus had proven resolute in His calling and in His willingness to lay down His life.

As leaders, we will all be tested in our use of authority, our sense of identity, and our desire for ownership. It's up to us to weigh and test the motives of our hearts. No one except for us will know whether this is a temptation that we have succumbed to. Jesus was resolute when He responded to the devil. What the devil was suggesting was not far off what was in His Father's heart, but He recognised the trap. He knew this was not the way He was to enter into what God had for Him.

Leadership temptations can be overcome, but we must not be unaware of the devil's schemes. The devil will always try to rob us of the greater potential God has for our lives. Let's choose to be led by the Spirit, not by the flesh. Let's be those who lead with a right perspective of ourselves and a sacrificial heart, knowing that when we partner with the strategies of God, we will achieve great things.

THE
LEADER'S TABLE

Dessert:

CHAPTER TWENTY-EIGHT

Don't Lose Your Hunger

Leaders stay fresh when they hunger after more of God because it continually pushes us out of our comfort zone.

In Luke 5, Jesus is preaching on the Shores of Galilee. When the crowd gets too close for comfort, Jesus steps into Simon's boat, tells him to push out from the shore, and from the boat, He preaches to the gathered crowd on the beach.

Simon had been fishing all through the night. Now it is daytime, and Jesus and a noisy crowd have turned up on *his* beach. He was busy washing the nets, finishing all his tasks. He was tired. He had done a whole lot of work and had nothing to show for it. He had caught *nada,* not one fishy fish. He was done, signing off. It was home time. Simon was planning to eat some bread with goat cheese and spend time getting reacquainted with his pillow.

But Jesus disrupts his plan.

Jesus needs somewhere to preach to the crowd. He has found His pulpit, and it's Simon's boat. Simon is stuck—Jesus has commandeered his boat. Now he has to listen to the preacher *and* look happy about it. This is the first time

Simon has met Jesus. He doesn't look anything special but there is something about Him, about the words He speaks, that resonates with Simon.

We don't know how long Jesus spoke for on that occasion, or what He taught. What is amazing is that while we don't know anything about His message that day, we do know that when He finishes speaking to the crowds, Jesus says to Simon and his friends, "Now go out where it is deeper..." (Luke 5:4).

Jesus knows they have empty nets, but understandably, Simon is reluctant. *Will it make any difference or will this simply be a waste of time?* He really just wants his bed. Yet for some reason, he does it. He puts back out to sea.

"Purpose trumps pillow"—that's what I often tell myself when I'm called to serve God over getting some sleep. Like Simon, we can be reluctant to forsake the call of comfort in order to go deeper with Jesus. Perhaps it seems like a waste of time and effort. It's not the direction we're used to travelling. It's easy to think pragmatically. *What's the next thing I have to do?*

Is going deeper with Jesus worth what it takes? Yes! In fact, as leaders, it's a price we can't afford *not* to pay. Going deeper is vital for developing our relationship with God and our understanding of Him. This is a great challenge for us as leaders. It is incredibly easy to stay in the shallows and never venture out to the deep places with God. But we can only access all of God by leaving the shallows behind.

When Simon gets out to the deep, Jesus tells him to let down the nets. Imagine what must have gone through Simon's mind. The nets are freshly washed and folded. The last thing he wants to do is start all over again. But Simon has seen 'something more' in Jesus. "Master," Simon replied, "We worked hard all night and didn't catch a thing, *but if you say so,* I'll let down the nets again" (Luke 5:5).

The truth is, Simon has to obey what Jesus asks before he can experience more of who Jesus is. Maybe this is also what we need to do. If we are to keep growing as a leader, we must let down our nets—our defences and walls, the way we see things—and open up to doing things Jesus' way. Leaders who are hungry are humble enough to hear what He says and obey it.

Simon heard the invitation of Jesus and obeyed, and what took place transformed him and his future. This time when he threw out the nets, they became full of fish, full to the point of nearly breaking! It was the wrong time of day for such a big catch, but this was the biggest haul of Simon's life—a miracle in the deep that he would never have seen in the shallows. From this point on, the gospel writers refer to Simon as *Simon Peter*. That day, God revealed more of Himself to Peter, and Peter's life was forever changed as he trusted God, ventured out into the deep, and witnessed His supernatural power.

The full nets are a symbol of overflowing blessing. This is what Jesus does in us when we go beyond the shallows—He takes us to a point where we cannot contain His goodness anymore. We are full to bursting with what He places in our hearts, in our lives.

Jesus asks leaders to go out where it is deeper, but many leaders live in the shallows (often feeding off the fish that other people caught). In the shallows is where the crowds are. For Jesus to cut through the noise in Peter's life, he had to leave the shore.

At the shores of our lives, the crowd is all we can hear. A shallow life is one where the crowd influences our values. We're meant to be a leader, but we begin to follow the crowd. We do what the crowd does, hear the voice of the crowd, and focus on our natural abilities and talents—the surface measurements of our lives. It's easy to feel satiated on the shores of leadership. That day, everybody on the shore had access to Jesus, but only those who launched out into the deep with Peter saw the miracle.

The shallows will leave us one-dimensional in our leadership, influenced by other people's learning and understanding. God wants to take us into another dimension—a deeper communion with His Spirit where we gain leadership revelation for ourselves. Hunger drives us beyond our understanding to the deep things of God. We only truly see His power and experience new depths of life in Jesus when we leave the shore behind.

Peter and his friends allowed their hunger to push them out deeper. There, they saw the miraculous power of Christ. A new abundance came to their lives, a new wonder. Until then, Peter had been self-assured, but that day, he saw his inadequacies. He saw the lack in himself—but even as that was revealed to him, he experienced Jesus' perfect love and acceptance. He experienced restored identity.

What the disciples experienced, we can too if we will just go deeper. Leaders have to lead from the deep place of meeting with God. We must stay hungry. Leaders who do this find they minister freely from an overflow of joy, freedom, and fullness of life in the Spirit. They find a new way of living, a freshness that sets them apart as leaders.

> *Blessed are those who trust in the Lord, and have made the Lord their hope and confidence. They are like trees planted along a riverbank, with* **roots that reach deep into the water**. *Such trees are not bothered by the heat or worried by long months of drought. Their leaves stay green, and they never stop producing fruit.*
> Jeremiah 17:7-8

Going deeper—however it looks, whether pushing out into the unknown or slowly sinking our roots into God—keeps us fresh. When we go deep, we are fruitful in every season. The deeper our pursuit of God, the deeper our inner stability and our assurance of who we are and who God is. Whatever happens in our lives, we can endure because we have chosen to go deeper.

As leaders, what we see in the natural matters less than what is happening in the unseen realm. This is how Paul lived victoriously while he was chained and held captive in prison. He had gone beyond his circumstances, beyond how others treated him, beyond his lack, to the position he held in Christ. He was able to write that he was not bound by his chains. Despite being in prison, he knew that he was raised with Christ and seated with Him in the heavenly realms (Ephesians 2:6 NIV).

When we go deeper, we see everything differently. God's love ruins us for the shallows. There is a fullness in Christ that satisfies the deepest longings of our souls.

> *Christ will make his home in your hearts as you trust in him. Your roots will grow down into God's love and keep you strong ... May you experience the love of Christ, though it is too great to understand fully. Then you will be made complete with all the fullness of life and power that comes from God.*
> *Ephesians 3:17-19*

In our leadership, we must remain hungry after God for two reasons:

Firstly, because that is where our identity as a leader is found. In the formative part of my leadership journey, I began to seek Jesus more intently. In that quiet place with Him, I began to weep and cry. Like Peter, I saw His worthiness and my unworthiness. For month upon month, every time I went deeper, I would cry. Then one day, after many months like this, there were no more tears. I had got to the end of me and begun to discover who I was in Christ. I was filled with an uncontainable joy—a joy that was deep and real. It was a transformation I could never have found in the shallows.

The other reason we must remain hungry for more of God is that there is hidden wisdom that leaders need that can only be found in the deep. 1 Corinthians 2:10 says, "For his Spirit searches out everything and shows us God's deep secrets." Like all of us, I find it easy to stay in the shallows and have to push myself to go out deeper. We so easily get caught in the noise around us, in natural ways of leading and in human wisdom. But it is in that deep place with God that we find the revelation, the answers, the understanding we need.

There is a personal cost to going deeper, but that is where the miracles are waiting. Oh that we would get so lost in the presence of God that we would be reluctant to return to the shore! Once we've tasted what God has for us in the deep, we will only long for more. As leaders, time is one of our more costly commodities, but if we take the time to go deeper, we will receive more than we could ever anticipate.

Peter was amazed by the supernatural catch of fish—but Jesus had something more in mind. "From now on you will be fishing for people," He said (Luke 5:10). Peter went out deeper with Jesus and the call on his life was clarified.

Do you know what it is to go deeper with God? To hear what Jesus has to say when you are away from the noise of the shallows? As leaders, we can only lead people where we have been ourselves. Keep pushing out to the deep. We will always come back with overflowing nets.

CHAPTER TWENTY-NINE

Expand the Kitchen

> *"It takes an army of talented and creative people to execute a successful restaurant."*
> — Callista Wengler

There's a reason why great chefs are often reluctant to let other people take over their specialty dishes and why famous restaurants and companies fiercely guard their recipes. It is because they want to remain unique and keep their edge in a competitive market.

This is opposite to how the kingdom of God operates. As leaders in the church and in ministry, not only do we need to be willing to give away our 'secret sauce recipe'—we have to be prepared to endorse the new chef and let everyone know that his or hers is the best sauce anyone has ever made (maybe even better than the sauce we were known for!). I truly believe that the more we give away, the more we receive. If we are stingy about letting others look good or reluctant to share what we have developed, we will make our world smaller and limit our ability to expand.

One key thing that always holds kingdom vision back, is finding people who can lead at a high level. It is frustrating for a leader when we see an opportunity to achieve more but we have no one equipped to do it. For the work God has given us to expand, we as leaders need to be able to move into new things—therefore, we need to raise up leaders who can confidently step up and do what we are doing. We need to set other leaders up with the authority to do what we have done. One of the most difficult things for those who follow us is to be given a job to do without being given the authority to actually get it done. Who wants to be an empty suit?

If we are unwilling to fully empower others to lead, this might be because:

- we know we can do the job well and it makes us feel secure;
- we have mastered our role and people admire us for that;
- being replaced makes us feel insecure;
- we are anxious about giving away something familiar in order to do something unfamiliar;
- we are unsure if we will succeed at the next thing (and if we fail, we fear that we may lose admiration and respect);
- we realise that when people begin to look to someone else as the expert, they will not be dependent on us anymore. (This is especially difficult if we struggle with co-dependency.)

Leadership expansion depends on letting others rise *and* do it better! Jesus said:

> "... anyone who believes in me will do the same
> works I have done, and even greater works,
> because I am going to be with the Father."
> John 14:12

To everyone's surprise and disbelief, Jesus was clear that He expected His disciples to not only do what He did but to do even more! This is mind-blowing! Jesus was *looking forward* to when others could do more than Him! This is the kind of leader Jesus is—He is releasing and empowering, not territorial or needing the accolades. Jesus was happy to pass on everything He knew to His disciples and encourage them that they would do even more than Him once He ascended back to heaven.

How many people are we surrounded with? Do we see the leadership role they could have? We need eyes to see. Jesus was surrounded by a crowd, but He was able to see twelve key leaders who would carry out His kingdom expansion after His ascension. But Jesus was not limited to only seeing and raising a small leadership team. He also empowered a group of seventy other leaders. In Luke 10:1-2 (TPT) we read:

> *After this, the Lord Jesus formed thirty-five teams among the other disciples. Each team was two disciples, seventy in all, and he commissioned them to go ahead of him ... He released them with these instructions: "The harvest is huge. But there are not enough harvesters to bring it in ... Now, off you go!"*

Jesus clearly saw that kingdom expansion required others to be able to do what He did. So often people sit inactivated because we only want them to do tasks—not to contribute to the bigger picture. We are happy for people to outwork *our* ideas, but not so sure we want *their* ideas and input. Expansion demands we let people move from outworking to owning the vision, to move beyond our delegated ideas to their ideation.

The early church had the capacity for expansion, not just because of the twelve, but because Jesus had empowered another seventy leaders. Jesus saw there was a labour shortage and that there was much work to be done—so He looked beyond His core group and activated others to carry the ministry.

As leaders, we are activators. Like Jesus, we are to identify, commission, and release leaders with clear instructions.

> "The harvest is huge. But there are not enough harvesters to bring it in. As you go, plead with the Owner of the Harvest to send out many more workers into his harvest fields. Now, off you go! **I am sending you out even though you feel as vulnerable as lambs going into a pack of wolves.**"
> Luke 10:2-3 TPT

Jesus sends the seventy even though they feel vulnerable. They may not have felt ready, but they *were* ready because of His anointing and call. It is the same for those we lead. Self-doubt and fears have to be dispelled for people to step up. Many times, people I am activating have said to me that they don't feel ready and they have proceeded to do a great job! Believing in and encouraging leaders is critical if they are to take on the challenge. But we must also give them authority.

> *Jesus replied... "Now you understand that I have imparted to you my authority to trample over [Satan's] kingdom. You will trample upon every demon before you and overcome every power Satan possesses. Absolutely nothing will harm you as you walk in this authority."*
> Luke 10:18-19 TPT

The most significant thing Jesus gave to the seventy was His authority. Because He gave them this, their words carried real weight and real power. They could transform people's lives!

As leaders, this is often why our activation fails—we call people, but we don't entrust them. When push comes to shove, are we actually willing to delegate real authority? When Jesus delegated authority, He was saying, "You being there is as good as me being there!"

> *Jesus concluded his instructions to the seventy with these words: "Remember this: Whoever listens to your message is actually listening to me. And anyone who rejects you is rejecting me, and not only me but the one who sent me."*
> Luke 10:16 TPT

Jesus didn't micromanage, He didn't check up on where the seventy were going and staying. He trusted them to work with what He had given them. What a result His empowerment generated. When the seventy returned, they were ecstatic! They were being used by God! Being activated and used by God is not ordinary—it's an overwhelmingly wonderful experience.

This wasn't the first group of seventy leaders to be activated in the Bible. Moses also activated a group of seventy leaders to deal with an expanding nation and a burden that was too big for him to carry alone. This also happened through an impartation:

> *Then the Lord came down in the cloud, and spoke to [Moses], and took of the Spirit that was upon him, and placed the same upon the seventy elders.*
> Numbers 11:25 NKJV

Moses and Jesus both gave instructions and imparted a supernatural mantle to a group of seventy people. Those they commissioned knew what was expected of them and they were given the spiritual authority to do it. If Moses hadn't given away a measure of authority to a group of leaders, he might not have had the time or space to climb the mountain and receive the Ten Commandments.

THE LEADER'S TABLE

In our leadership, what we are doing now may be the very thing we need to give away. God is calling us to the *next thing* He has for us. Our reluctance to empower others will not just hold up their destiny but also our own. If Moses had stayed only in the role of judge, he would not have stepped into one of the greatest roles in history.

If the burden is too great or the work we are doing is not expanding, we must look for the twelve, look for the seventy, look for the leaders around us that can receive an impartation for bigger things.

Have you ever thought about what happened to the seventy leaders Jesus commissioned? Was this moment of wonder and activation the height of their service? Not at all! The impartation they received changed their lives—and the church—forever. Their personal expansion was permanent, and their kingdom impact, eternal.

I find it incredible that many of the seemingly random people that Paul mentions in his letters were among the seventy Jesus sent out (see Romans 16:8-14, 19-23). Look at what some of them are believed to have gone on to become:

- Ampliatus became the Bishop of Bulgaria
- Stachys became the Bishop of Byzantium
- Aristobulus brought the gospel to Britain
- Herodian became Bishop of Iraq (Neoparthia)
- Phlegon became Bishop of Marathon in Thrace
- Hermes became Bishop of Dalmatia
- Patrobas became Bishop of Neapolis (Naples)
- Hermas became Bishop of Philippopolis
- Jason became Bishop of Tarsus
- Sosipater became Bishop of Iconium
- Tertius became Paul's letter writer and Bishop of Iconium after Sosipater

- Erastus became a minister and deacon in Jerusalem
- Quartus became Bishop of Beirut

Wow! The seventy formed a leadership framework. They became the bishops and leaders of the early church. When Jesus first sent them, He didn't just have a one-off ministry trip in mind. These people enabled the church to spread around the region and they continued to change the world! Many of them, according to church history, were martyred for their faith. The Bible and church history give accounts of what sixty-nine out of the seventy went on to do for God. What a legacy—the wider the call and empowerment, the greater the kingdom expansion. These seventy were more than servants, they were leaders and contributors and world-changers! As leaders, when we give away authority, we reap a vastly increased harvest.

What recipes have you developed over the course of your ministry? Have you prepared others to step into your shoes? We have to teach emerging leaders the skills they need to succeed. They need to know how to run a great meeting, how to build an enduring culture, how to preach and communicate well, how to get people on board with vision, how to create a sustainable ministry model. They need to be taught how to pray for healing, how to minister in the power of the Holy Spirit, how to hear from God, how to choose a team, and how to be discerning. The skills that we have acquired over many years and through successes and failures are now ours to give away.

When we release people, we must impart spirit, vision and anointing. What's in us can be on them! Moses had to release another tier of leadership to get Israel ready to take possession of the promised land. Jesus had to release and activate another tier of leaders to see the kingdom of heaven expand.

There are four keys to 'expanding our kitchen' and releasing leadership:

1. See the need, see the new opportunity. See the person or people who could be part of the expansion.
2. Call people to do the work. Your endorsement of them and confidence in them will allay their fears and encourage them to embrace the next level of leadership.
3. Give real power away. Be willing to not just pass the baton but to throw a mantle over others. Give away ownership. Empower leaders to innovate and create, not just replicate. As Pastor Ben Naitoko once said, "You don't see Jamie Oliver's managing McDonalds." If we want other great chefs to run the kitchen besides ourselves, we need to give them the freedom to come up with their own menu.
4. Release people to go to places we have never been. See them grow in their sphere of influence and ministry. The ultimate goal is not only that leaders are released but they in turn become the ones who see, call, give, and release. The seventy went where Jesus hadn't been and would never go. This is how we go from adding to multiplying. This is kingdom multiplication. This is true expansion.

Drawing from the twelve tribes of Israel, Moses appointed seventy elders and he had a fail rate of *two*. Only two of those Moses appointed didn't work out. Jesus sent out seventy disciples and he had a fail rate of *one*. Pretty good result, really!

As leaders, we can take heart. If some of the people Moses and Jesus entrusted leadership to experienced failure, so will we. Don't worry if some of the people you appoint aren't able to fulfil the role. Unfortunately, from time to time, that will happen. But the success rate is going to be much higher than the fail rate.

We must be committed to releasing and activating leaders. We will see far more people succeed than we thought possible. What are you waiting for?

EXPAND THE KITCHEN

It's time to hang out the 'help wanted' sign. The workers are too few. Expand the kitchen at all costs.

CHAPTER THIRTY

Roasting Fish, Restoring Leaders

Jesus has been recently resurrected. What does He do? He stops by the shores of Galilee to cook Peter fish for breakfast (John 21).

Jesus' first order of business is to make a meal and restore Peter to leadership.

What an amazing picture! Our resurrected Lord, cooking fish and bread over a charcoal fire on the beach and inviting the guys to brunch.

It is a picture of unhurried humility. The Lord of Life is bending down, cooking for them, waiting on them. The heart of Christ, even after His resurrection, is to serve and work for our freedom.

He lights a charcoal fire on the beach. The smell of the charcoal fire evokes a memory for Peter. The last time Peter stood around a charcoal fire was in the High Priest's courtyard where three times he denied being a follower of Jesus.

Peter feels the shame, the regret.

He had told Jesus, "I will always stand with you." He had believed that he would hold the line no matter what, but when Jesus was arrested and the crowd turned against Him, fear got the better of him. He betrayed Jesus by denouncing Him publicly.

Peter is angry with himself for not being stronger. He resents what happened; he wishes he had reacted differently, spoken differently, not been weak.

Instead of getting it together, instead of leaning on the mercy of Jesus, he has gone back to his old life. He has gone back fishing, full of shame.

Shame makes us retreat and pull back. Shame stops us from being who we are meant to be.

There may be a moment when a leader fails. There are leaders who regret the mistakes they have made and long to be restored. Jesus wants us to confront the shame and break it off their lives.

Peter has to learn how the restoration power of the cross can work in his life. Jesus has to get him to confront the shame and receive His love and mercy.

We have to learn how to restore leaders. We see how to do this in the way Jesus roasts fish and restores Peter. They share a meal together. They reconnect around the warmth of the fire and food. Jesus gives Peter the time to build rapport before the restoration starts. He uses the table to show acceptance, create connection, and bring a challenge.

Jesus wants to challenge Peter and see him restored to leadership, but only after He has shown a relational commitment to him. As leaders, there are times we need to bring a challenge, but we are to do it relationally. We often need to have the small talk before we can have the real talk.

In his sermon, *Listening to Jesus Beside the Sea,* Charles Swindoll describes the importance of how Jesus treats Peter:

> "A significant failure usually means termination or demotion. That's the way the world works. But not the kingdom of God

... After Peter's dismal failure in the courtyard, humility displaced his bravado. Jesus took His emptied, forlorn disciple back to the beginning."

Jesus is bringing Peter full circle. "Follow me," He says, just as He had in the beginning. Jesus is giving Peter a fresh start, a restoration of grace, an invitation to follow God again. I imagine their relationship was even deeper and richer because of this interaction. Instead of being written off and rejected, Peter has been lovingly corrected and re-appointed.

Jesus is the great restorer and redeemer. He died for our mistakes. For *all* of them. Yet so many Christian leaders live unrestored.

> Cooking is the art of adjustment.
> – Jaques Pepin

If people were to come to us, would they find grace and a willingness to restore them? How much do we believe in the grace of God? Do we truly believe that people who have failed can start again? Is there a statute of limitations on what God can forgive and what He can restore?

The most important thing we must realise when we restore someone is that failure is not final. As leaders, we must guard against welcoming repentance and encouraging restitution but not allowing for restoration. God never leaves us in our failures. He always has a plan for us to get back on track.

How do we restore people? We can only restore people if they are willing to trust us. Restoration requires exposing the most vulnerable part of one's soul to another. Exposing our failings is hard.

We must approach those we lead with the view that they are clay in the Potter's hand, and as such, they are on a journey of becoming who God has purposed them to be. We approach them with love and respect, no matter what has been broken in their life. Their honesty can lead to their breakthrough. True restoration occurs when we believe God still has a future for that person.

As leaders, we need to know how to restore people. There are a few basic steps:

1. Discern the root issue behind the sin or struggle. When Jesus asked Peter, "Do you love me?" He was reaching beyond Peter's behaviour and speaking to his heart. He was showing Peter that love can drive out fear.
2. Create an opportunity to listen.
3. Name the problem. Jesus sometimes said to the demons who were bothering people, "What is your name?" (Luke 8:30 NIV). Most often a person knows what the real problem is—or at least they can see part of it. Naming issues is vital if a person is to be victorious and free at the core of their identity.
4. Create opportunities for a new confession.
5. Encourage people towards their future. Your words have creative power. When someone has opened their heart to you, be very purposeful about sowing the right seed.

When dealing with unforgiveness, offences and betrayals, we must take care not to end up in the judgment seat. God's will is always that people get free, healed, whole, released and recommissioned.

Jesus shows us that taking time to restore people is a vital investment. It's what leaders do. After this encounter with Jesus, Peter became a catalyst for the spread of the Gospel. Over breakfast, he got his breakthrough. In one morning, Peter went from stagnation to a fresh surrender, from failure to freedom, from shame to confidence. Once again, he left his nets and followed Jesus.

Is there someone who needs you to cook them breakfast?

CHAPTER THIRTY-ONE

A Legacy Dinner

Don't you find it annoying when guests turn up late to dinner? The meal starts to burn, the meat dries out, the kids are no longer well-behaved angels because they are hungry and just want their dinner... But if Jesus was the guest, I'm sure He would be excused. He can turn up whenever He wants to! I don't think any dinner party could beat the one where Jesus decides to turn up unexpectedly (although King Belshazzar may disagree—he certainly did not enjoy the sudden handwriting on the wall at his dinner!).

After the resurrection, the disciples have gathered for a fish-fry meal when Jesus turns up, unannounced.

> *Jesus himself was suddenly standing there among them...*
> *They stood there in disbelief, filled with joy and wonder. Then*
> *he asked them, "Do you have anything here to eat?" They gave*
> *him a piece of broiled fish, and he ate it as they watched.*
> Luke 24:36-44

Andrew and James have to be thumped on the back by Matthew and John to dislodge the food they are choking on as Jesus suddenly appears out of the blue, giving them the fright of their lives. Jesus must have thought they looked hilarious with their mouths hanging open, their forks poised mid-air. This is the first time they have laid eyes on Jesus since His death.

> *As they were eating together ... he told them, "Go into all the world and preach the Good News to everyone."*
> Mark 16:14-15

He gets straight to the point. Jesus has turned up, interrupting the disciples' dinner, to dish up a plan for the future of the church.

It was transition time.

This was the ultimate legacy dinner, a true 'dinner for days'. He was giving instructions to the apostles. After this meal, there would be no room for doubt or confusion. They would know what to do. They were to share the good news.

Jesus made His expectations and expansion plans clear while they ate. The message of salvation was being entrusted to them. They were to take this hope to the nations.

This wasn't the only time Jesus turned up. Jesus met with them many times post-resurrection. He focused on making sure they knew what to do and that they had everything they needed to fulfil their mission.

> *During these encounters, he taught them the truths of God's kingdom realm and shared meals with them.*
> Acts 1:3-4 TPT

As their bodies were fed for the day, their mind and spirit were simultaneously equipped for what was to come. Jesus is spiritually preparing the disciples with a store of information regarding the kingdom of God. He is making sure they are aware of the power He is investing in them, and He is transitioning them to carry authority on the earth in His absence.

This investment Jesus makes with His apostles gives us a blueprint for the development of legacy, how to hand over well. He has tested and approved His group of leaders, He knows that they have competence and aptitude, and He is putting the gift of the gospel message into their hands. His release will be absolute.

He is transitioning; He is headed to His next assignment in heaven, and He is leaving the Church on earth in their hands. To see the Father's kingdom come on earth is now going to be their responsibility.

Handing over well, managing transitions, and succession planning are big questions for leaders to resolve—what does it look like to give someone else what you have carried? From Jesus' example, it involves:

- Explanations
- Teaching
- Encouragement
- Clarity
- Impartation
- True release (not partial but full entrustment)

So many leaders seem to struggle with handing things over. Often, they do not really release responsibility or they take the entrustment back off their leaders before they've had a chance to succeed.

Jesus empowered the apostles by giving them a clear mandate without giving them a game plan. They knew the goal, the purpose and the importance of their task, but they didn't have to do it a set way.

Sometimes a leader trying to create ministry continuity actually stifles their legacy by putting too much of themselves into the future plan and allowing too little room for the person assuming the responsibility. Jesus knew the apostles had to be truly and authentically themselves in order to do what He needed them to do. Kingdom expansion wasn't going to eventuate through following a list, but by following the Spirit of God and His leading as they brought their full self to the task of advancing the kingdom.

This is how we should pass on our ministry legacy also. Leaders must commit to serving a 'dinner for days'. Like Jesus, we need to impart clear purpose and vision while empowering our next leaders with tremendous freedom to take the legacy forward in a way that is true to them. Maybe they will no longer do it 'the right way'. It is hard as leaders when people take what we've done and change it. But that's the only way to truly release leadership; it's the way it has to be if the legacy is to continue even stronger than before. In releasing others, don't dump and run. Don't become absent or hard to reach. They may very well still need your encouragement and support.

I remember John and I sitting around a brunch table with Pastor Paul de Jong in New Zealand. He was talking about how he had approached the handover of Life Church, the church he had established, to his successor. "Transition is about when they are ready, not when you are ready," he said. He went on to explain that the next season in God is ready when the people taking it over are ready. "There may be aspects of leadership transition that feel hard to navigate, but the transition won't be as difficult for you if you can see what God has ahead for you."

I love this perspective. Leadership transition isn't about our readiness to let go, but the next leader's readiness to take it on. What a reversal to the way we often think leadership transitions should play out. If there is someone who is ready to lead, it might be time.

When we are the leader transitioning out of our role, it does not mean we are no longer a visionary person. The vision we have never dies, it just changes. Transition is not the end of our vision, it's the beginning of a new one. God wants us to serve Him till our last breath.

As leaders, we want to build a legacy that continues long after we have left.

A LEGACY DINNER

*One generation shall commend your works to
another, and shall declare your mighty acts.*
Psalm 145:4 ESV

Let's continue to do life, share meals, talk about the kingdom of God around tables, and wait with bated breath to see what God will do through the generations to come. It will be so much greater than we can imagine.

CHAPTER THIRTY-TWO

It Begins and Ends... with Dinner

As leaders, we must never forget that the way Jesus leads us is to first share a meal with us.

> *"If you hear my voice and open the door, I will come in and we will share a meal together as friends."*
> Revelation 3:20

His leadership of us begins with a meal and it ends with a meal. Before He departs from the earth, Jesus promises us He will not drink from the grapevine again until we are joined with Him in heaven at the wedding feast of the Lamb. This is the occasion our bridegroom has been waiting for—the heavenly arrival feast where, yet again, we are all invited to dinner! The concept of dining with us is never going to go away.

Why will Christ always value the table?

Because He is relational.

Because He works transformationally.

Because He calls us friends.

We are not a duty or a burden to Christ. We are His great joy!

The same is true of the people we lead. Paul wrote, "Dear friends, you are my joy and the crown I receive for my work" (Philippians 4:1).

A leader should always be found around the table. Kingdom life will overflow as fellowship overflows. Leading in a way that others linger will transform their lives—and ours as well.

Acknowledgements

To John, thanks for endless hours of listening to me talk about this book and constantly cheering me on. Don't worry, I've got the next book to talk about now...

To Lara and Will, the best kids in the world. You have always 'got' ministry, the hours, the sacrifice, the service. Thanks for being part of this ministry journey with us. To Joshua Lin, we love you and think the world of you.

To Anya, Jeff and the Torn Curtain team, thank you for making this book better in every way. Anya, the hours of working collaboratively not only finely honed the manuscript, it was a beautiful time together I will always treasure.

To Nathan Chambers, thank you for the incredible cover art, you're an anointed genius.

To Jürgen and Leanne Matthesius, thank you for being true friends, and for your generosity, wisdom and kindness in our lives. We love you both and all our Awaken family!

To those who so generously endorsed this book, thanks for your love and belief in me.

To Mum and Dad, thankyou for being the best parents a girl could ask for. You have given me so much and I've been so blessed to have you both. You have always worked to set me up to win in life and been a great example to me. You showed me the importance of the family dinner table, and Mum you are my favourite chef! You guys are the greatest and I love you.

To Alan and Irene, you are two precious gems. You have been great cheerleaders and your consistent love for me has been an undergirding support all these years.

To my family, the Stewart's, Cameron's, Miller's and Salembeni- Stewart's. Love you all! I never take for granted the joy and laughter we have whenever we are together. Near or far we are always together in spirit.

To Chris Runciman and Simon Greening, thanks for being in our corner when we needed you.

To Jack and Ashya McDonald, thanks for cheering me on at all times. Jack for being one of the first to give me feedback on the book and be genuinely excited about it. Ashya, I thank God for you every day, we are living our best life together, every minute with you is endless joy.

To Dave and Bex Connett and Karolina Grant, your friendship and encouragement have meant the world to me.

To Pastor Tak Bhana, thank you for being a source of encouragement and bringing the word of the Lord to me when I needed it most.

To Ross and Kathy Abraham and our INC friends. Thank you for your friendship and partnership.

To Pat Cunliffe, thanks for helping with the audio recording and being the right person at the right time.

To the Arise Leadership Team we led. Thank you for your love, fidelity and hard work. Teamwork makes the dream work. We did amazing things together and we love you all so very much. Nathan Chambers, Melvyn Tan, Ben Carroll,

Brent and Annie Cameron, Abby Ayling, love you guys. To the Campus Pastors, thank you for leading so well and being full of faith.

To Aidan & Anna Dorfling, Caleb Ayling, Anna Chambers, Anna Carroll, Adam and Berni Johnson, Joel and Suzy Norris, Kristy-Lee Lasei Faitaua, Courtney Poutoa, Nath and Deb Seiuli, Ray and Emma Moore, Michael and Dorcas Adjeisasu, Dynes and Ingrid McConnell, Dan and Rautini Tiaiti, Dave and Jenny Gilpin, Ed and Vic Bamford-Bryant, Harry and Annaliese Slade, Rochelle Jackson, Chelina Roberts, Tim Ng, Bradley Page, much love now and always.

To all past and present Arise Church staff and members—you are always in our hearts and in our prayers. Thank you to all those who we served the Lord with, and we look forward with joy to all the good work that will stand the test of time being revealed on our Lord's return.

About the Author

Gillian Cameron is in demand for her preaching and also for her in-depth leadership insight. Her preaching is clear, passionate and anointed. Her prophetic ministry has impacted many believers and churches. Gillian has trained a great number of Christian pastors and leaders and has equipped many others to enter full-time ministry. For bookings or enquiries, reach out through the website.

Empower Leader

Empower Leader, led by John and Gillian Cameron, exists to coach pastors and leaders, to ensure that church leaders have all they need to minister effectively and fruitfully, and to bring momentum and revival to the church in our generation. Their vision for the body of Christ is that the Church would be revived and grow, that souls would be won, that pastors would be strengthened and resourced, and that together God's people would be empowered and equipped to build the church. If you would like to be part of a coaching cohort or connect with what Empower Leader can offer, please visit the website for further details.

www.johnandgilliancameron.com

Made in the USA
Columbia, SC
11 June 2025